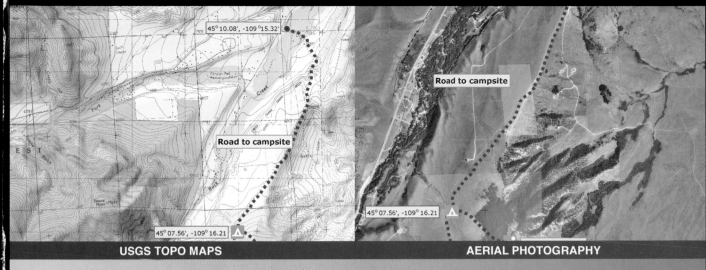

Stoeger Publishing
Great Outdoor Books Since 1925

STOEGER PUBLISHING COMPANY IS A DIVISION OF BENELLI U.S.A.

BENELLI U.S.A.
Vice President and General Manager:
Stephen Otway
Director of Brand Marketing and Communications:
Stephen McKelvain

STOEGER PUBLISHING COMPANY
President: Jeffrey Reh
Publisher: Jay Langston
National Sales Manager: Cheryl Crowell
Managing Editor: Harris J. Andrews
Design & Production Director:
Cynthia T. Richardson
Photography Director: Alex Bowers
Imaging Specialist: William Graves
Sales Manager Assistant: Julie Brownlee
Editorial Assistant: Christine Lawton
Administrative Assistant: Shannon McWilliams
Proofreader: Celia Beattie

Published by Stoeger Publishing Company
17603 Indian Head Highway, Suite 200
Accokeek, Maryland 20607

BK0306
ISBN: 0-88317-250-X

Library of Congress Control Number: 2002110078

Manufactured in the United States of America.

Distributed to the book trade and
to the sporting goods trade by:
Stoeger Industries
17603 Indian Head Highway, Suite 200
Accokeek, Maryland 20607
301-283-6300 Fax: 301-283-6986
www.stoegerindustries.com

OTHER PUBLICATIONS:
Shooter's Bible 2004 - 95th Edition
The World's Standard Firearms
Reference Book
Gun Trader's Guide - 26th Edition
Complete Fully Illustrated
Guide to Modern Firearms with
Current Market Values

HUNTING & SHOOTING
Elk Hunter's Bible
Shotgunning for Deer
The Turkey Hunter's Tool Kit:
Shooting Savvy
Hunting Whitetails East & West
Archer's Bible
The Truth About
Spring Turkey Hunting
According to "Cuz"
The Whole Truth About
Spring Turkey Hunting
According to "Cuz"
Complete Book of Whitetail Hunting
Hunting and Shooting
with the Modern Bow
The Ultimate in Rifle Accuracy
Advanced Black Powder Hunting
Hounds of the World
Labrador Retrievers
Hunting America's Wild Turkey
Taxidermy Guide
Cowboy Action Shooting
Great Shooters of the World

COLLECTING BOOKS
Sporting Collectibles
The Working Folding Knife
The Lore of Spices

FIREARMS
Antique Guns
P-38 Automatic Pistol
The Walther Handgun Story
Firearms Disassembly
with Exploded Views
Rifle Guide
Gunsmithing at Home
The Book of the Twenty-Two

Complete Guide to Modern Rifles
Complete Guide to Classic Rifles
Legendary Sporting Rifles
FN Browning Armorer to the World
Modern Beretta Firearms
How to Buy & Sell Used Guns
Heckler & Koch:
Armorers of the Free World
Spanish Handguns

RELOADING
The Handloader's Manual of
Cartridge Conversions
Modern Sporting Rifle Cartridges
Complete Reloading Guide

FISHING
Ultimate Bass Boats
Bassing Bible
The Flytier's Companion
Deceiving Trout
The Complete Book of Trout Fishing
The Complete Book of Flyfishing
Peter Dean's Guide to Fly-Tying
The Flytier's Manual
Handbook of Fly Tying
The Fly Fisherman's Entomological
Pattern Book
Fiberglass Rod Making
To Rise a Trout

MOTORCYCLES & TRUCKS
The Legend of Harley-Davidson
The Legend of the Indian
Best of Harley-Davidson
Classic Bikes
Great Trucks
4X4 Vehicles

COOKING GAME
Fish & Shellfish Care & Cookery
Game Cookbook
Dress 'Em Out
Wild About Venison
Wild About Game Birds
Wild About Freshwater Fish
Wild About Waterfowl

Photo(opposite):
Courtesy of Larry Weishuhn

Elk Hunter's Bible®

by Jim Zumbo

STOEGER PUBLISHING COMPANY, ACCOKEEK, MARYLAND

CONTENTS

INTRODUCTION

I wish I could say that I learned to hunt elk from a mentor who was a veteran woodsman, a person who taught me at a young age about elk and elk country. Unfortunately, that wasn't the case.

My first efforts in the elk woods began in the mid-60s, when I tried my best to find an elk on public land in Utah. For six years my pals and I hiked steep slopes, crawled through thickets, and sat on lookouts, but none of us ever pulled the trigger. Admittedly, there weren't a lot of elk in Utah in those days, but enough so that more fortunate hunters managed to take elk almost every year. Most of those folks had permission to hunt private land where most of the elk lived. I was frustrated. I vowed to learn everything I could about elk. I wanted desperately to tie my tag to an elk—any elk—cow, spike, or mature bull.

I succeeded, but it was a long, tough, uphill trail. Along the way I met plenty of wonderful folks who were willing to share their elk hunting wisdom. I began applying for elk tags in other states, and focused on elk in every habitat possible. I wanted to know how they behaved in lower elevations, in high country, and places in between. It became a passion for me, and I never grew tired of elk and elk hunting.

I'm fortunate to have hunted in every western elk state, as well as many mountain ranges and wilderness areas. But after more than 30 years of slipping around in elk country, I'm still learning. I'll continue to learn, and I'm sure I'll keep making mistakes. As they say, experience is the mother of learning. There's no substitute for having "been there and done that."

In this book, I've tried to present elk and elk hunting in a way that will hopefully be of some value to beginners and veterans alike. I take an in-depth look at the animal—how it behaves, its food and breeding patterns, how, why, and where it travels, and, of course, strategies to hunt them. For those hunters who don't live in elk country, I've included basics on planning a hunt beginning with where to go, how to obtain tags, what gear to bring, camping options, transporting an elk out of the woods, getting the meat home, and a lot more.

Far more hunters, both resident and nonresident, go home without an elk than those who do. While I can't guarantee that you'll tie your tag to an elk if you read this book, it's my hope that you'll be better prepared.

A hunter once asked me for advice on being a successful elk hunter, requesting that I sum it up in one sentence. Here was my reply: learn as much as you can about elk, hunt every hour of the day, especially the first and last few minutes of shooting light, get as far away from roads and people as you can, and hunt smart. If you do that, you'll have a far better chance of seeing your magnificent quarry, and ultimately ending up with a freezer full of the finest wild game you've ever feasted on. And if you don't bring home an elk, rest assured you'll still have plenty of memories that will last a lifetime. Elk have a way of doing that to you.

I'm fortunate to have hunted in every western elk state, as well as many mountain ranges and wilderness areas.

THE HISTORY OF ELK IN NORTH AMERICA

Elk gather at a winter feeding station in the National Elk Refuge in Jackson, Wyoming. Elk were trapped and transplanted here from other areas around the country in the early 1900s.

There are four subspecies of elk, including this Tule elk from California. Erroneously called the "dwarf elk," animals on prime habitat are anything but small. This bull weighed 825 pounds live weight.

ACCORDING TO historians, elk made their way to North America via a land bridge that connected Alaska to Siberia some 10,000 years ago. That land bridge is the Aleutian Islands now, which resulted when the ice receded after the ice age, when much of the north was connected by glaciers, ice, and snowfields.

Because of their Siberian ancestry, elk found North America to their liking and spread throughout the United States and parts of Canada. They inhabited many different environments, from eastern hardwood forests to the mountains of the West, as well as the prairies and lowlands. Tolerant of cold because of their Siberian ancestry, elk adapted best to the high country and latitudes where low temperatures prevailed.

The early 1900s was a dismal period for North American wildlife. There were few wildlife agencies that regulated hunting, and wildlife numbers were severely depressed. The last of the passenger pigeons was wiped out, buffalo were on the road to extinction, and people marveled at seeing a deer or elk track. Market hunting and the absence of game laws invited wholesale slaughter. Animals were recklessly killed for their meat, fur, and antlers, and, in the case of elk, for their teeth as well. Elk have a pair of unique teeth called ivories that were in high demand for fashion purposes, and countless animals were killed for them. Then too, since elk competed with cattle for forage, they were targeted by settlers who saw elk as competitors.

There's a popular notion that elk were driven into the mountains by settlers, and that's why they're basically mountain animals now. That's not true. Elk were always in the mountains; they were simply harder to hunt than the easier animals on the prairies. Lowland elk were wiped out first.

Luckily, some farsighted individuals became concerned over the plight of America's wildlife. It was too late for the passenger pigeon, and the slaughter of buffalo was finally stopped. Newly formed wildlife agencies, both state and federal, began enacting laws to protect what wildlife remained and to assure their future. Hunting seasons were designed to permit the taking of animals that produced a surplus each year, and many species could not be hunted at all.

Because of an abundance of predators that were perceived to be a major problem, agencies declared an all-out war, putting bounties on their heads. In a fairly short time, wolves were wiped out of the West, grizzlies were eradicated from the western states except for parts of Wyoming and Montana, and coyotes, mountain lions, and bobcats were hunted year-round by government hunters. Given the political attitudes of that era, as well as the concerns over dwindling wildlife, predator control was considered to be appropriate and necessary.

Less than 50,000 Rocky Mountain elk were left after decades of slaughter, down from an estimated 10 million elk that roamed North America when the country was settled. Most of the remaining animals inhabited the National Elk Refuge adjacent to Jackson, Wyoming,

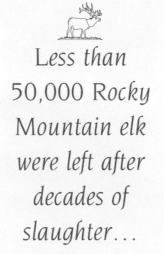

Less than 50,000 Rocky Mountain elk were left after decades of slaughter...

and in Yellowstone National Park. In the rest of the West, they were just about wiped out, except for some remnant herds. There were remaining small populations of the other three subspecies, the Roosevelt, Manitoba, and Tule elk. Because of protection, they were able to maintain populations and subsequently thrive. Unfortunately, that wasn't true for the Eastern and Merriam's subspecies, which became extinct.

Roosevelt elk live in western coastal forests from northern California to Alaska. Because of the density of the forests they live in, they were able to maintain small populations. Their numbers rapidly expanded as they were protected by new game laws.

Tule elk inhabit only California. According to historical records, only two animals, a bull and a cow, had survived the massive overhunting. They lived on a ranch, and were zealously guarded by the landowner. Those two animals became the core of an entire new population, and now more than a dozen areas in California support more than 3,000 animals. By decree of the California legislature, Tule elk can never be established outside state borders.

Manitoba elk managed to hold their own in Canada and were also seriously depleted by overhunting. Again, new game laws paid off, and healthy herds now live in Canada and North Dakota.

To ensure the survival of the Rocky Mountain elk, conservation leaders initiated a massive transplant program. Thousands of elk were captured in

This bull issues a challenge in typical elk country: a beautiful high mountain land that is remote and inaccessible to all but the hardiest people.

A bull wades in flooded bottomland somewhere in the West. Elk populations in the United States and Canada are now at all-time high and occupy more suitable habitat than at any time in the last hundred years.

Yellowstone and in the Elk Refuge and were shipped throughout the country by rail and trucks. This was a monumental effort, and it worked. Tiny transplanted herds began to blossom, and elk tracks could once again be observed in much of their original range in the West. A few herds became established in the East, but nothing to compare with the large numbers of Eastern elk that were the original inhabitants.

As the years passed, elk numbers exploded, thanks to restrictive hunting laws, continued transplant programs, and efforts by organizations such as the Rocky Mountain Elk Foundation. Today, there are about 900,000 elk in the West, and new herds are being established east of the Mississippi. For example, Wisconsin, Kentucky, Arkansas, and North Carolina have new populations of animals that are thriving and doing so well that limited hunting has been allowed. Obviously, the big animals are here to stay, provided we can protect the critical habitat they need for survival.

ELK COUNTRY

Most elk live in high mountain country, but significant populations also reside in habitats as diverse as western piñion and juniper forest and eastern deciduous woodlands.

PLEASE KEEP OFF GRASS

Piñon-juniper forests occur throughout the central and southern Rockies, but many hunters ignore them in favor of traditional elk habitat. In fact, elk thrive in these forests.

THERE'S A common perception that elk country is exclusively mountainous, timbered terrain laced with creeks and rivers, overlooked by towering, snow-capped peaks. That's largely true, but much elk habitat doesn't fit into that category.

Wild elk inhabit every western state, and several states east of the Mississippi. The term "wild" is necessary to set apart domestic animals in pens that are kept in virtually every state. In the West, where the vast majority of elk live, mountain country is indeed the primary elk habitat. It's there that elk roam over millions of acres of timbered slopes, much of it on public land.

The U.S. Forest Service administers 191 million acres of land in national forests throughout the country, most of them in the West. Within those forests, many wilderness areas have been established by the U.S. Congress, all of them off-limits to any kind of wheeled travel, and internal combustion engines, ruling out chain saws and generators.

Where national and private forests contain commercial timber, logging operations are common. Areas where timber has been removed are called clear-cuts, and are often magnets for elk, since they offer abundant and nutritious forage not found in the timber. Clear-cuts are often vilified by people who oppose the cutting of large sections of forests, but it's a well-documented fact that logged areas produce lush vegetation that elk prefer to eat.

Many western forests have natural clearings, called "parks," containing native grasses. Elk feed in these extensively, since grass forms a large part of their diet. Burned areas are also attractive to elk, since fires create conditions that produce lush vegetation. In most mountain country, water is usually available in drainages that support year-round waterways, so animals aren't required to travel long distances to drink as in more arid areas. Except for wilderness areas where roads are prohibited, most public forests are well roaded, offering plenty of access to elk country.

Forests are classed into different "types." The nature of each type of forest depends on various factors, such as latitude, elevation, soil characteristics, water availability, slope exposure, and others. In mountainous country, the very highest elevations may be above tree line, where low-growing willow and other tough plants eke out an existence in this very hostile environment where the growing season is only a matter of weeks.

Elk live in this high country in the summer and early fall when deep snow doesn't cover the forage base. Alpine forests grow at the highest elevations Typically, the spruce-fir type is here, trees that can withstand severe winters and brutal growing conditions. They are said to be the "climax" type, since they're the last in the succession chain. Below them in elevation we commonly see Douglas fir and lodgepole pine types, or a combination of both.

Then there are the ponderosa pine and quaking aspen types at even lower elevations. Finally, the piñon pine and juniper make up the lowest forests. These two species do very well in arid conditions. The very lowest habitat is typically high desert, commonly composed of sagebrush and various shrubs. Elk range throughout these habitats depending on the time of year, climate, and availability of food. For example, you might find plenty of elk in the alpine area early in

the fall and very few elk in the lowlands. Elk will seek the cooler heights and shun the hot lower elevations. When deep snow covers the high country, however, you'll do well to find an elk in the upper reaches. They'll be in the lower areas where food is more available.

Elk migrate to winter ranges when snow forces them down. These are critical areas, many of them zealously protected from developers. Wintering areas are used by elk year after year. This part of elk country is seldom hunted, since few hunting seasons run late enough. Typically, the seasons are over before elk return to the lower, more accessible habitats.

Outside the West, elk range from hardwood forests in North Carolina and Arkansas to more than two-million acres of revegetated coal mines in Kentucky.

Elk dwell in an amazingly complex mosaic of habitats, from the highest alpine to deserts. And it's all good. Just the presence of elk makes it special.

We usually consider elk country to be high in the snow-capped peaks, but elk live in many environments, such as this lowland cottonwood forest.

ELK BIOLOGY

Here is a classic example of food preferences. The mule deer in the foreground is feeding on sagebrush, a standard dietary preference, while the elk in the background is eating grass.

Elk have excellent vision and can see long distances, as many hunters have learned the hard way.

SENSES AND FOOD PREFERENCES

Sometimes I think elk have exceedingly acute senses, and sometimes I think they're as dumb as fence posts. The difference is the time at which I'm observing them, as well as the hunting pressure. During the rut, elk are concerned with breeding, and both sexes are primarily concerned with reproducing their own kind. Bulls are especially distracted, having only one thing on their minds, and that's mating with as many cows as possible.

To that end, bulls sleep and feed little, and aren't acutely aware of danger when they're actively interacting with cows and other bulls. Their senses seem to be dulled to the point where they're extremely vulnerable. I've seen bulls and cows approach humans so closely that you could almost touch them, but that was during the height of the rut.

Bulls that are solo are more cautious, since they don't have cows and other bulls to deal with. However, that doesn't mean herd bulls aren't wary. They'll spook instantly if they see, hear, or smell danger. Many hunters who pursue elk in the rut know that herd bulls can be difficult, if not impossible to call in, but that's often because the bulls are protecting the cows they've gathered, perhaps by refusing to respond to the hunter, or by running away with the cows. That may be senses at work, but I believe it's more an instinctive mechanism to procreate with numerous females.

Look at this cow's ears. She's at full alert after having heard something she didn't like. She may soon give a bark if she's fully alarmed.

18

Elk that are constantly on the alert for hunters in areas of heavy hunter pressure have an extremely high intolerance of people. When they need to, they can tune up their senses to the point where they're as wary as whitetails. I've seen elk spook a quarter mile away when they saw humans, and I've seen them explode from their beds in heavy timber when they heard a foreign sound.

Their noses are as good as any other members of the deer family and they can detect odors at several hundred yards. I've seen many elk become alarmed at 400 yards or more when the wind suddenly switched and blew my scent toward them.

The eyes of most mammals are different from those of humans. We don't see very well in the dark, and not at all on a black night, but animals can indeed see well. Most of them, in fact, are nocturnal. On the other hand, we can see color, but animals don't. They see in shades of black and white. This is due to the makeup of the eye, which consists of rods and cones.

Rods accept ultraviolet light, and cones detect color. Since animals have more rods than cones, their night vision is superb, but their color perception is poor. We humans are just the opposite, with more cones than rods. Color is not a problem for us (though some people are colorblind), but we have terrible night vision.

I'm convinced that no matter how bright or reflective the color, an elk will not suspect that it represents a form of danger unless it moves. That's how we can get away with wearing bright orange when an elk is staring us down. As long

This bull scrounges for food on the forest floor. He is probably looking for mushrooms, which are preferred during certain times of the year.

Fire has always been a natural event in the forest, and elk have little fear. Fire actually increases forage over the long term.

ELK HABITAT

HABITAT
- Remote mountainous heavily timbered environments
- Mixture of forest, dense cover, and grassy clearings (parks)
- Local water source

ROCKY MOUNTAIN ELK
Evergreen (spruce, Douglas fir, Alpine fir), Hardwood (quaking aspen), Southern Rockies (piñon and juniper), Colorado, Utah, New Mexico, Arizona high-desert summer habitat (sagebrush, scrub oak, piñon and juniper)

ROOSEVELT ELK
Northwestern rain forest: evergreen (firs, cedars, hemlocks, spruce, pine), hardwoods (red alder, maple)

ELK FOOD PREFERENCES
- Grasses: wheatgrass, brome, bluegrass, fescue, timothy
- Forbs: wild geranium, peavine, lupine
- Browse: bitterbrush, serviceberry, ceanothus

as we don't move, the animal will be likely to ignore us.

The senses of one elk to determine danger are formidable enough, but consider the awesome ability to detect enemies when the animals are in a herd and all those eyes, ears, and noses are working together. Being very social animals, elk are seldom by themselves and have plenty of company to warn of impending peril.

When we see a picture of an elk in a magazine, it's usually in a lovely glade or meadow where there's a carpet of lush grass. Most of those photos are taken in the fall, when elk are feeding heavily on grass. The reason the animals are in the open at all is because that's where their menu is. Many grass species are sought out, but favorites are timothy, wheatgrass, bluegrass, brome, and fescue. Grass simply grows best in the sun. Because freshly logged-over areas and old burns have had the timber canopy removed, nutritious forage generally grows there, offering a smorgasbord for elk and other wildlife. These are great places to scout when you're looking for elk feeding areas.

But that's not always the case. In many areas, grass grows fairly well in timber if the soil is rich and well aerated, and enough sun shines on the forest floor to satisfy the light requirement of grass. In places where there's sufficient grass in forests, elk may not come out of the timber to feed, especially if there's significant hunting pressure.

In the winter, elk will paw through snow to reach grass underneath, requiring more forage to generate sufficient calories to allow them to withstand the cold. Though most elk migrate to lower elevations and spend the cold months on winter ranges, some stay at intermediate elevations where constant wind blows away the snow and exposes grass on those windswept ridges.

In the very highest elevations, elk must leave before the truly deep snows blanket the alpine landscape, because their food is virtually unavailable. In some of that high country, four to five feet of snow is common, with much greater depths where the snow drifts and piles up to 10 feet deep or more. Obviously, no grass-eating animal can survive in that arctic environment.

Grass isn't the only forage eaten by elk, and in fact, it makes up less than half their diet in many areas. They also consume large amounts of browse and forbs. Browse consists of shrubs, such as aspen, willow, ceanothus, serviceberry,

and bitterbrush. These species are some of their favorites. Forbs include dandelions, lupine, peavine, and wild geranium, among others. In the winter, elk may nibble on the bark of aspen trees.

During periods of stress in severe winters elk are often fed by people in traditional wintering areas. They may survive the winter because of these contributions, which usually consist of hay and alfalfa, though grains are sometimes fed as well. The most famous wintering area is the National Elk Refuge in Jackson, Wyoming. During the winter, upward of 10,000 elk are fed by federal employees. The public can ride a horse-drawn sled out to the elk and observe the animals at close range—so close that wild elk may nibble on your boots.

Elk are classified as ruminates. They have a unique stomach consisting of four parts – the rumen, which is where the unchewed food is temporarily stored, and the other three parts that process the food afterward, known as the reticulum, the omasum, and the abomasum. This four-chambered stomach is present in all members of the deer family. Like other members of the deer family, elk chew their cuds during the day after feeding much of the night. Biologists believe this behavior is due to the animal's instinct of eating quickly,

This herd of elk rests in a sagebrush environment. Since they live in herds, it's difficult to sneak up on them.

This bull has large antlers for three reasons —food, genetics, and age. Nutrition is important in growing large antlers.

storing the food, and converting it to a digestible form during the day when they can watch for enemies. Otherwise, they would be more vulnerable when they were feeding in the open.

If you want to win a trivia contest, ask your hunting pals whether elk have front teeth only at the top of their mouth, only at the bottom, or both. The answer is only at the bottom. The animal tears the food between its lower teeth and roof of the mouth and swallows it, only to chew it later as part of the digestive process. Elk also have an "ivory" tooth on each side of the mouth that has no known function. These teeth

Elk prefer grass much of the year, but will eat many other browse species as well.

are highly regarded as fashion objects, and are made into rings, earrings, pendants, and other items of jewelry. Both cows and bulls have "ivories," but those of the bull are almost twice as large as a cow's. The most preferred ivories are those that are darkly stained, especially if they have a pattern of concentric rings. The dark coloration comes from the food they've been eating.

The feeding habits of elk depend on the degree of pressure that they're under from hunters, the availability of forage, and the season, which ultimately determines the type and amount of forage that elk have access to. Because food may be completely covered by snow in higher elevations, elk migrate each year to traditional winter ranges that have been used by the same herds for years and years.

On a daily basis when elk aren't under pressure, they feed very late in the afternoon, on and off during the night, and very early in the morning. Where they're consistently disturbed, however, they'll often head for the timber long before legal shooting hours, often in the dark when it's just getting gray in the eastern sky. They may not come out to feed again until it's dark or in late afternoon, when shooting hours are over.

This spike wears his first antlers ever. Practically every bull starts off his life with straight spikes, though there might be some variations with a very small fork or two.

AGE, SIZE, AND ANTLER GROWTH

All male elk need three elements to grow large antlers—good genes, nutritious and sufficient forage, and age. Of the three, age is the most important. A bull elk may have the best ancestry on the mountain, and plenty of quality forage, but if he doesn't survive several hunting seasons to reach maturity, he won't be old enough to grow large antlers. In places with heavy hunting pressure, bulls seldom live more than two hunting seasons. This is especially true on public land where there's good access. Bulls are taken so consistently that very few escape to produce a decent six-point rack.

The biggest bulls come from places where there is limited hunting pressure, such as backcountry or wilderness areas, private lands where hunters are restricted, or limited entry units. Each year, enough bulls are able to survive to older ages. One very well-documented bull lived to be 25 years old in the wild. He was tagged in Wyoming in 1913 when he was a spike and transplanted to Arizona. A hunter killed him in 1937.

Cows live longer than bulls for two reasons. First, they don't get as stressed during the breeding season as bulls do. During that time of year, bulls eat very little and are focused only on mating. They lose weight rapidly and, if an early winter occurs, they are among the first elk to die because they're in poor condition. Second, when cows are hunted, which is very frequent because of the need to keep elk herds trimmed, old cows are seldom distinguished from younger cows since they don't wear antlers. A percentage of the cow population will survive many seasons, and it's not uncommon for a cow to be 10 years old or older.

When elk are born, calves will weigh about 30 pounds. Studies show that they'll gain weight at the rate of about one to two pounds per day until they're several months old. As yearlings, they may weigh 200 pounds or more, with the spikes being heavier than cows. In every case, bulls far outweigh cows of the same age class. As bulls get older they continue to gain weight, and when they're mature and in pre-rut condition, they may weigh upward of 800 pounds live weight, though 650 to 700 pounds is the average. Cows in good condition will weigh 500 to 550 pounds. A big bull will stand five feet or more to the top of the shoul-

Tule elk ... were once known as "dwarf" elk because of their small size...

der and will be eight feet from nose to tail.

Those are the average weights of the Rocky Mountain subspecies, but the Roosevelt elk of the West Coast is decidedly heavier, with big bulls approaching 1,000 pounds or more. Interestingly, the rain forests in which these giants live are steep, slippery, and extremely dense. Packing the meat of a mature bull out of this nasty country can be the biggest ordeal in all of elk hunting. Tule elk, which live only in California, were once known as "dwarf" elk because of their small size, but that was because the elk that were studied and weighed lived in poor habitat. Where Tule elk live in good habitat, they'll weigh in excess of 800 pounds. In every case, the heaviest elk will be those that are not only mature but also live in places where there's plenty of quality forage.

A biological term called "Bergman's Rule," states that mammals living in the northern latitudes are bigger in body size than those of the same species living in more southerly latitudes. The theory suggests that the larger body size in the North allows less heat loss during very cold weather, enabling animals to survive arctic conditions.

This is easily demonstrated with deer and moose, but in the first two decades of the 1900s, elk were transplanted from Wyoming to most places they currently inhabit. This was done to reintroduce populations to places where they were virtually extirpated. Because those Wyoming elk have lived only 80 years or

This bull is in his glory, having survived several hunting seasons. He's at least five years old and will be a dominant bull during the upcoming breeding season.

so in their new environments, adaptation has not occurred, and an elk in southern Arizona may be as big as an elk of similar age in northern Idaho.

Elk hunters love elk for many reasons, with antlers being one of the primary factors. A big bull is a lovely creature to behold, with long, massive antlers that carry six points on each side of the rack. A bull begins his journey to adulthood by growing spike antlers during the second autumn of his life. During the first autumn he's a calf and has no antlers. Spike antlers are usually single appendages that grow upward with a slight curve, but some may have a small fork or even an extra small point on one or both sides. Most are between 15 to 20 inches long, but they can be as long as 24 inches or more. Quite often spike antlers are still encased in velvet, which normally falls away from the antlers of older bulls by the time breeding season arrives.

The spikes give way to so-called "branched antlers" the following spring. These bulls will have racks that typically have four or five points to the side. In marginal habitat, these antlers may be fairly small, but will often be quite robust in good habitat. Bulls of this age are commonly referred to as "brush bulls" or "raghorns." They're sexually mature, but they have a way to go to attain their full size.

As the bull grows older, his antlers increase in mass, beam length, and tine length. In most cases, six points to the side is the norm for a mature bull. Hunting writers have coined the name "royal" for a six-point bull, "imperial" for a seven-point bull, and "monarch," for an eight-point or better bull, but these aren't chiseled in stone, and, in fact, no one knows who came up with them.

The antlers of a mature Rocky Mountain or Manitoba bull have well-defined tines that grow off the main beam in an orderly fashion, but the antlers of Tule elk or Roosevelt bulls often have a "crown" on top where the three top points grow close to the end of the beam. This is also true of the red stag, which is related to our elk.

The first tine on a six-point rack is called the brow tine or eye guard. The second is the bez or bay, and the third is the trez or trey. The fourth point is called the royal, dagger, or wolf point and is typically the longest tine. The fifth is called the sur-royal, as is the sixth point, which is actually the end of the main beam.

If a spike survives another year, he may look like this bull, often called a raghorn. He's 2 1/2 years old and isn't fully grown, but is sexually mature.

To make a quick, field evaluation of a bull, look at his royal points. If they appear to be 15 inches long or longer, you're looking at a nice bull. Size up the other tines as well, especially the third point which is usually the shortest. If you're looking for a typical Boone & Crockett bull, you'll have your work cut out for you. These monsters must score a minimum of 375 points and only handfuls are taken each year.

These wonderful antlers appear in the spring, usually in late April and early May, just after the old pair is discarded. They grow rapidly, and by late July and early August are fully grown. As they grow, they're encased in a soft covering called "velvet" which protects them during this very fragile period.

By late August, the velvet falls away, and the new antlers are red. They turn white in a few hours, and attain a dark color as the bull rubs them on brush and saplings. Contrary to popular belief, the velvet isn't purposely rubbed off but is discarded naturally. The bull takes on saplings as part of his breeding ritual. Soon he will use those antlers to impress cows, and bluff or fight other bulls. Then we show up, looking for the bull of our dreams.

WHERE TO HUNT ELK

A State-by-State Directory

THIS DIRECTORY covers the nine major elk states in the West where the bulk of elk hunting is done. States that require a major stroke of luck to draw a tag (such as Nevada) aren't included, nor are states that don't allow nonresidents to hunt (such as California and South Dakota). There are also small numbers of elk found in a few parts of Alaska and in the midwestern and eastern states, where very few tags are issued and in most cases, nonresidents can't hunt.

ARIZONA

This southwest arid state is known for deserts and heat, but it's also the place to go for a truly monster bull. Textbooks say the last Merriam's subspecies was killed here in the early 1900s, which may explain the huge elk. Merriam's elk had very large antlers, but were hunted relentlessly, allegedly to extinction.

Curiously, the last Merriam's elk was supposedly wiped out during an era when there was no agency to compile a census of elk populations. There were no wildlife managers or biologists, just observers. It is currently believed by some scientists that not all the Merriam's were killed off and that the survivors interbred with the Yellowstone elk that had been transplanted from Wyoming. Whatever the case, Arizona produces bulls that make grown men drool.

You don't need to be rich to hunt these monster bulls, though that can be the case if you wish to hunt one of the famous Indian reservations. National forests offer super bulls

where an outfitter isn't required, since there's often good access and forgiving terrain.

Unfortunately, your odds of getting a license for a public land hunt aren't good. You must compete in a very competitive lottery, and it might take years to obtain a tag. Residents and nonresidents alike must compete for lottery tags. To increase your odds, Arizona offers bonus points. Of course, the more points you have, the better. Obviously, the top units are the toughest to draw.

Finding a place to hunt is not difficult because plenty of big bulls live in national forest land. If you aren't familiar with the state, draw a circle 50 miles around Flagstaff, and you'll enclose much of the best elk country in Arizona. The highest elk densities are in the southern part of Coconino County, with excellent public hunting

MAP KEY

National Forest

Prime Elk Hunting

National Park

Wildlife Refuge

ARIZONA
Elk Population:
50,000
Highest Density:
Southern Coconino and Apache counties

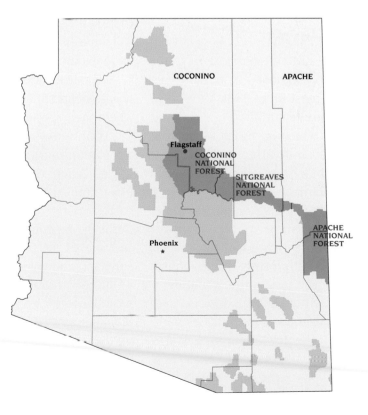

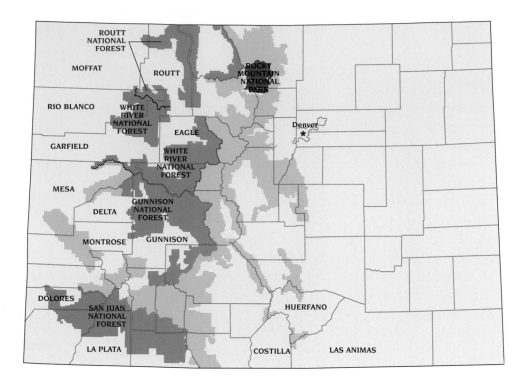

in the Coconino National Forest. There are also high densities of elk in the southern part of Apache County, with good public hunting in the Apache-Sitgreaves National Forest. Currently there are about 50,000 elk in Arizona.

COLORADO

This is the premier elk state in terms of the very highest elk populations and the largest annual elk harvest. At least a quarter million elk inhabit Colorado, which is about 25 percent of all the elk in North America. It's not uncommon for hunters to take 50,000 or more animals annually.

Colorado offers preference points that help hunters obtain hard-to-draw limited entry tags. Of course, the better the hunting, the tougher it is to draw the tag. In the top units, it might take more than a dozen points to be eligible for a permit. Colorado is one of the few remaining states where nonresidents can still buy a general tag over the counter.

There are several firearms elk seasons in the state, their length depending on the season. Archery seasons are early in the fall, and there's a special muzzleloader season. Many hunters prefer the last firearms season because there's a better chance of snow that will drive elk out of the high mountains and into the lower elevations.

It's safe to say that elk are now firmly entrenched in Colorado's mountains where they were originally found when the country was settled. The highest populations are found in most of Routt, Eagle, Delta, Gunnison, Dolores, La Plata, and Costilla counties, and in the eastern parts of Moffat, Rio Blanco, Garfield, Mesa, and Montrose counties, as well as in the western parts of Huerfano and Las Animas counties.

Public hunting is available on national forests and Bureau of Land Management (BLM) land, with some of the best hunting on the Routt, White River, Gunnison, and San Juan national forests.

COLORADO
Elk Population:
250,000
Highest Density:
Routt, Eagle, Delta, Gunnison, Dolores, La Plata, and Costilla counties; eastern Moffat, Rio Blanco, Garfield, Mesa, and Montrose counties; western Huerfano and Las Animas counties

IDAHO

This is an excellent elk state, with elk roaming everywhere except for the southern agricultural regions. There are plenty of national forests and BLM lands that permit public hunting. Some of Idaho's quality elk habitat is disappearing because forests there are maturing and, as a result, forage is decreasing, but on the whole, Idaho's 110,000 elk will continue to provide excellent hunting.

Idaho offers a limited quota of tags to nonresidents that are available on a first-come, first-served basis. Hunters who are first to apply get their tags. A number of limited entry units offer an outstanding opportunity at a trophy bull, and there are plenty of wilderness areas that offer good hunting, such as the Selway Bitterroot Wilderness Area. Firearms seasons vary according to the region and herd units, but there are some superb September hunts in wilderness areas and in some limited entry draw areas.

The highest densities of elk are found in parts of Shoshone, Clearwater, and Idaho counties, but there are also good populations in the northern Panhandle and in parts of Adams, Boise, Valley, Lemhi, Elmore, Camas, Clark, Fremont, Bingham, Bonneville, Caribou, and Bear Lake counties. Look to the Clearwater, Nez Perce, Salmon, Targhee, and Caribou national forests for very good hunting.

MONTANA

The Big Sky State is one of the best, with plenty of elk in mountain ranges, from the western to eastern borders and parts in between. Most elk, however, are found in the west, in the Rocky Mountains or in smaller ranges east of the Rocky Mountain front. About 95,000 elk inhabit Montana. In most of the state, a five-week general firearms season allows hunting from late October to Sunday of Thanksgiving week. Many veteran hunters don't bother hunting until the last week,

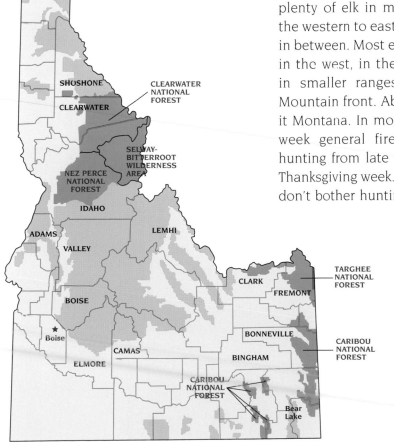

IDAHO
Elk Population:
110,000
Highest Density:
parts of Shoshone, Clearwater, and Idaho counties; northern Panhandle; parts of Adams, Boise, Valley, Lemhi, Elmore, Camas, Clark, Fremont, Bingham, Bonneville, Caribou, and Bear Lake counties

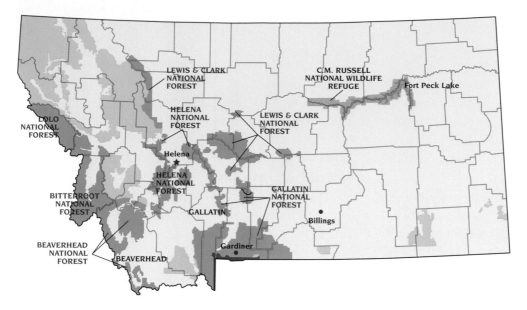

MONTANA
Elk Population:
95,000
Highest Density:
in the west, in the Rocky Mountains or in smaller ranges east of the Rocky Mountain front. Also in Gallatin, Beaverhead, Lolo, Bitterroot, Helena, and Lewis & Clark national forests

when there's a better chance of snow moving elk into the lower elevations.

Nonresident general tags are available in a lottery, but outfitter tags are offered to those who wish to have a guided hunt. There are some excellent limited entry tags available, notably for the C.M. Russell Refuge around Fort Peck Lake, and for very late hunts around Gardiner, near the northern boundary of Yellowstone National Park. The latter are four-day hunts for bulls, with seasons extending into February. This unit is one of the best in the west for big bulls that are accessible to the public.

Elsewhere, there is good hunting on the Gallatin, Beaverhead, Lolo, Bitterroot, Helena, and Lewis & Clark national forests, though there is good hunting on the forests in Montana. Plenty of BLM lands also offer good public hunting.

NEW MEXICO

This southwestern state is known for big bulls, though some of the best come from private lands that typically are expensive to hunt. New Mexico offers several hunts for firearms hunters, all of them lasting for five days. Only one hunt can be selected.

New Mexico has a unique system that allots tags to landowners, depending on the amount of land they own and the size of their elk herd. The landowner may then sell the tags, either directly to hunters, or to outfitters. There are also several Indian reservations that offer outstanding hunts for trophy bulls, but these are also very expensive. For the hunter who can't afford high-dollar hunts,

NEW MEXICO
Elk Population:
50,000
Highest Density:
in the north-central region; also in the southwest; Rio Arriba, Taos, Colfax, Los Alamos, Mora, Catron, McKinley, Sandoval, Santa Fe, Lincoln, and Otero counties

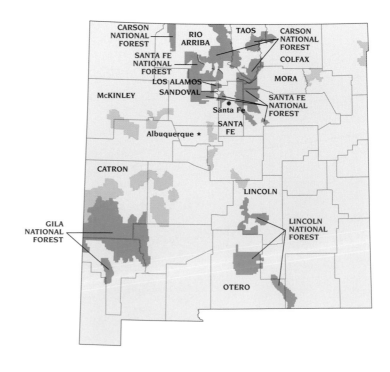

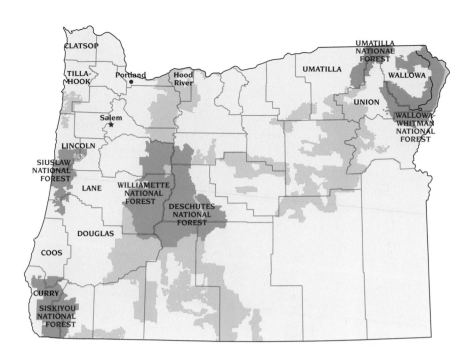

there are plenty of good public land hunts on national forests as well as BLM lands.

Elk herds are scattered, with heaviest densities in the north-central region, and also in the southwest. In the former, look for high concentrations in Rio Arriba, Taos, Colfax, Los Alamos, and Mora counties. In the southwest, elk herds are highest in the western portion of Catron County. There are also good numbers in parts of McKinley, Sandoval, Santa Fe, Lincoln, and Otero counties. The Carson and Santa Fe national forests are prime places for public hunting in the north, while the Gila and Lincoln offer fine hunting in the more southerly areas. For its size, New Mexico doesn't have a huge herd. About 50,000 elk inhabit this state, but many of them have trophy potential.

OREGON

Both the Rocky Mountain and Roosevelt elk subspecies inhabit Oregon, which is second only to Colorado for the size of its elk herd. About 120,000 animals roam this northwest state. Oregon boasts some huge bulls, with many on limited entry areas. Many general seasons allow spikes only, with branch-antlered bulls available to those who draw tags. A preference point system is in place to offer better odds to draw.

Roosevelt elk live in the most rugged habitat in North America. This region, which extends from the coast inland, has extremely steep slopes covered with heavy timber and underbrush that may literally defy human travel. It is rainy country, and hunters who take an elk here by hunting the forest have achieved a commendable accomplishment. Good concentrations of Roosevelt elk exist in every coastal county, from Clatsop county that borders Washington, all the way down to Curry County that borders California. The Siuslaw and Siskiyou national forests offer excellent public hunting, though many large timber companies allow access as well.

Because of the difficulty of hunting the coastal forests, many hunters head to the more central or eastern regions. Some of the largest herds live in Hood River and all of Lane County, but the highest density herds are in Umatilla, Union, and Wallowa counties in the northeast. There is good public hunting on the Deschutes and Willamette national forests, and in the northeast there are plenty of elk on the Umatilla and Wallowa-Whitman national forests.

UTAH

Elk herds in this state have exploded in the last 20 years, with about 60,000 elk roaming within, as compared to 25,000 in 1980. Utah has outstanding limited entry areas where lucky winners in the lottery contest can try for the bull of their dreams. Utah offers bonus points that allow a way to beat the odds in the drawing system

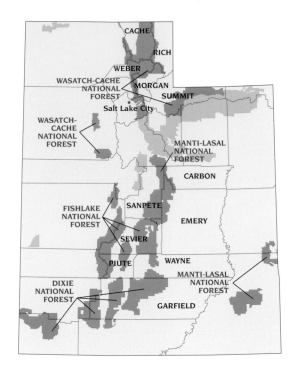

UTAH
Elk Population:
60,000
Highest Density:
Cache, Rich, Weber, Summit, Morgan, Sanpete, Carbon, Emery, Sevier, Piute, Wayne, and Garfield counties

ties, and all of Morgan County. In the south, elk are at their best in parts of Sanpete, Carbon, Emery, Sevier, Piute, Wayne, and Garfield counties.

The Wasatch National Forest in the north is a great public area with good access throughout much of it, and in the south, look to the Manti-Lasal, Dixie, and Fishlake national forests. Public lands are crowded in Utah. Hunters who score consistently get away from crowds, either on horseback or by walking. For those who want a wilderness adventure, the high Uinta Mountain range that borders Wyoming on the north offers very remote hunting.

There are also landowner tags available, but these are fairly expensive, as well as some Indian Reservation hunts.

Virtually all of Utah's mountain country is inhabited by elk, and there are plenty of animals in the lower elevations characterized by cedar forests. Lowland BLM areas also harbor good elk populations. The highest concentrations are in the north and south-central regions. In the north, look to parts of Cache, Rich, Weber, and Summit coun-

WASHINGTON

Like Oregon, Washington also offers the Roosevelt and Rocky Mountain elk subspecies. Roosevelt elk inhabit the western portion of the state, from the seacoast inland toward the Cascade Mountain range. Many hunters pursue elk by watching for them in clear-cuts where visibility is good. Relatively few people will actually penetrate the

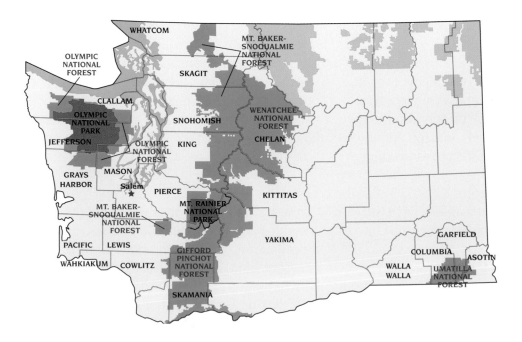

WASHINGTON
Elk Population:
60,000
Highest Density:
Jefferson, Clallam, Grays Harbor, Mason, Wahkiakum, Pacific, Cowlitz, Pierce, Lewis, Yakima, Kittitas, Walla Walla, Columbia, Garfield, and Asotin counties

34

WYOMING
Elk Population:
150,000
Highest Density:
Teton and Park
counties

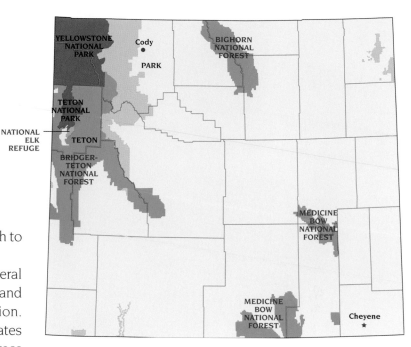

horrid jungles of soggy, slippery brush to hunt elk.

Hunters must select one of several regions where they intend to hunt, and must stay only in that region. Washington is one of the few states where nonresidents can buy a tag across the counter. Bonus points are offered to help beat the lottery odds.

In the west region, elk populations are highest in parts of Jefferson, Clallam, Grays Harbor, and Mason counties in the northwest, and in Wahkiakum, Pacific, and Cowlitz counties. The Olympic and Gifford Pinchot national forests have good densities of elk. In the central area, parts of Pierce, Lewis, Yakima, and Kittitas counties have high numbers, and in the southeast the most elk inhabit parts of Walla Walla, Columbia, Garfield, and Asotin counties. The Mt. Baker-Snoqualmie, Wenatchee, and Umatilla national forests provide excellent public hunting. A number of timber companies also allow private access.

Statewide, there is a population of about 60,000 elk in Washington. Hunter success for general hunts is among the lowest in the west, perhaps because Washington is the smallest western state with the second highest human population and rapidly disappearing habitat.

WYOMING

This state consistently offers the highest hunter success rate, which is typically around 40 percent. Elk inhabit all the mountain areas, with the heaviest populations concentrated in the

northwest, notably in Teton and Park counties. There are also good elk herds in the Bighorn Mountains in the north-central area and in the Medicine Bow area in the south. Currently about 150,000 elk inhabit Wyoming.

Excellent limited entry units offer outstanding hunting where hunter success is 75 percent or better. Wyoming doesn't offer preference or bonus points for elk—everyone has an equal chance of drawing a tag. Nonresidents must draw a tag in a highly competitive lottery, even for a general unit hunt. Wyoming is one of the few states where no landowner tags can be purchased. Application deadlines are among the earliest in the west, allowing hunters who don't draw the opportunity of trying other states.

Elk seasons vary with the units, and since the state micromanages big game by having management objectives for each herd, there are over 100 units and 100 different season structures. Many seasons open in early October and run for about three weeks. One of the best hunts begins in mid-November and runs into early December. It's a trophy bull hunt that's offered in half a dozen units around Cody. There are also some unique hunts in and around the National Elk Refuge and in Teton National Park near Jackson

PLANNING THE HUNT

It takes plenty of planning and homework to put together all the details in order to be a successful elk hunter.

The end result of a well-planned hunt is plenty of fine meat.

ANY HUNTING

trip should start with a plan. One of the toughest things about elk hunting is figuring out how to put it together. Planning is vital, especially if you intend to hunt on your own. But even if you decide to hire an outfitter, you'll still need to decide on a plan. Elk hunting is especially complicated because it typically occurs in a very unique habitat that you probably aren't used to if you're not a resident of the West. Here are animals that reside in higher elevations that you may not be accustomed to, and in large tracts of steep, timbered areas where there are few roads. Small wonder that an elk hunt could be a major mystery that leaves you in the dark.

The very first decision is to select your hunting companions, unless you plan on going solo. Choosing your hunting pals is an important part of the planning process. If things don't go as well as you hoped they would, it's good to have a buddy who thinks like you do and will take things in stride. Many hunts have gone sour because two people couldn't get along and had uncomfortable disagreements. If you are going solo, never plan a two on one hunt with an outfitter, allowing the outfitter to pair you up with a stranger. This could be a catastrophe if you and the other hunter have clashing personalities.

The most important part of the hunt is where to go. That's obvious, because you need to be in a place that not only has elk, but the kind of elk you hope to bring home.

The best way to resolve the where dilemma is to go with a pal who is familiar with a good hunting spot. If he can't go with your party, he at least can steer you to a good place. If no one in your party has any inkling of where to go, you'll have a profound challenge if you're headed to elk country on your own.

The first thing you need to do is pick a state. Before embarking on this project, be aware that every state has widely differing regulations pertaining to license availability. For example, California is the most discriminatory state against nonresidents: they can't hunt elk there, period. In some states, such as Nevada and Arizona, even residents must apply for an elk tag, along with nonresidents. Some states, like Idaho, offer a quota of tags to residents that are distributed via a first-come, first-served system. Most states require non-residents to draw a tag in a lottery.

Of the top elk states, Colorado is an exception. Nonresident general elk tags are unlimited; hunters may buy them in department stores or from any licensed dealer. Consider, too, that Colorado, like other states, requires hunters to have a hunter safety certificate if born after a certain date. It becomes immediately obvious that some states have passed an array of confusing regulations. To figure them out, get online or write or call the agency and check the rules. Make sure your applications are in well before the application deadline, and make sure you understand when the application must be received.

Some states require your application to be physically received by the deadline, while others consider the deadline to be the day you mailed it. In most states you can submit party applications. For example, if three of you will go hunting, you can submit one application—either you all draw or none of you draws. Don't interpret party hunting to mean that you can shoot your pal's elk or vice versa, as you can do with deer in a couple states. That type of party hunting is a serious law infraction in every elk

Each hunter must shoot his or her elk and no one else's.

state. Each hunter must shoot his or her elk and no one else's.

Every state offers limited entry hunts, and most offer a so-called "general" season. The latter means you can hunt anywhere in the state where units are open to unlimited hunting. Some states, like Arizona and Nevada, have no general seasons—all must be drawn for specific units. The limited entry unit is simply an area where a quota of tags is established to distribute hunter numbers. Typically, these units offer high-quality hunting, often on public land where there's good access and above-average bulls. For obvious reasons, the very best units are the toughest to draw.

Many states have a point system that allows you to improve your odds of drawing. They are either preference points or bonus points. Preference points accumulate over the years, and you're assured of a tag once you acquire the appropriate number of points. For example, let's say you want to start earning points. You send in the appropriate fee for the tag along with your application, and select unit 1 as your preferred unit. If you don't draw, you'll get your money back, minus an application fee, which is normally under $5, and you'll have a preference point. You repeat the process the following year and receive another preference point. Eventually you will have collected enough points for unit 1. If five points are required for a tag, you'll have a guaranteed tag when you have accumulated five points. Of course, the top units will require the most points. A bonus point

This hunter gave an elk hunt to his son for his graduation gift. Wise planning helped him put it together.

is simply an extra application with your name on it. If you have three bonus points, you have three applications working for you. Unlike the preference point system, you won't be assured a tag if you persevere, but you might not have a long wait. You may draw with only one bonus point.

Let's assume that you've drawn a tag, or you'll hunt a state like Colorado where you can simply buy one. That done, you'll need to roll your sleeves up and actually find a place to hunt if you have a general tag and you aren't going with an outfitter. If you're absolutely clueless about where to go, call the state wildlife agency and get pointed in the right direction. There are 191 million acres of national forests in the U.S., with the majority of those lands in the West. Elk inhabit much of that acreage. The Bureau of Land Management has 270 million acres in the U.S., with elk living on BLM land, chiefly in the higher elevations.

Generally speaking, of the 11 western states, only California does not allow nonresident hunting. Though Nevada has some tremendous bulls, only a couple dozen tags are offered to nonresidents in a highly competitive draw. That leaves the remaining nine to choose from. Alaska has some elk and there are very limited elk hunts in a handful of other states. As I mentioned, a big hurdle is simply getting a tag, Colorado being a notable exception.

You must make a choice based on your own expectations regarding the basic type of hunt you want. Do you simply want to bring home some excellent elk venison, are you looking for a big bull, will you settle for any bull, or are you interested in a backcountry hunt where you won't be bothered by other hunters? All these factors must be carefully weighed. If it's meat you're after, all the nine states offer cow tags. In some, you can take a second elk per trip, which must be a cow. Be aware that some states require you to take

Do your homework before the hunt and make sure you have updated maps.

only a spike bull with a general tag in most units. You must draw a lottery tag to take a branch-antlered bull.

If you'll be satisfied with any bull, do some homework to learn about places that offer decent hunter success rates. Doing a backcountry hunt on your own is a major undertaking. Not only must you have the appropriate gear, but you'll also need to be in good enough shape to haul your gear on your back, assuming you're hiking and not riding horseback. Then again, you must have the means—and the brawn—to be able to pack the meat out. A wilderness area is by far the toughest. It will be far from a trailhead, and no modern conveyances are allowed.

If you aren't willing to hunt with crowds, then think twice about hunting in a general unit, especially in a popular elk state like Colorado. In my home state of Wyoming, public lands have far fewer hunters simply because the quota of nonresident tags is regulated. Hunter success rates are very high, as are the

chances of seeing a good bull on any national forestland. Once you've selected a place you want to hunt, contact the government agency that administers the land and buy a map. If you're camping, check the locations of campgrounds close to your hunting area and make sure they're still open.

It's possible that you might find a place to hunt on private land. Make no mistake—in popular elk states most ranches are closed to casual public hunting. That wasn't the case in the early 1960s when I moved west. Most ranches were open to hunters. A telephone call or knock on the door was all it took. Those times changed when landowners began to realize that their wildlife was an asset and that hunters were willing to pay good money for permission to hunt.

Planning also assures that you bring the appropriate gear. Make a list so you'll pack all the essentials. Little things may become major headaches if you forget them. For example, if you have no replacement mantels for your gas lantern and the mantel in it isn't functional, you might be in the dark for a long time. If you forget your axe, firewood for the wood stove may be wishful thinking.

Don't underestimate the difficulty of getting your elk out of the woods. This can be a very big problem—pun intended—because elk are big animals. Imagine trying to move a 600-pound or heavier carcass. You'll need to cut it up and get it to a road, often over very rugged terrain. The best elk hunts are those that run smoothly. You can't control the weather, or the behavior of the elk, but you can control the selection of your hunting spot and accommodations. Do your homework, and you will indeed have a far smoother hunt.

ELK ON A BUDGET

A small tent and a willingness to rough it will allow you to hunt on a budget and get away from other hunters.

An elk hunt can be easily affordable if you go with a couple of buddies, but be prepared for any unforeseen misadventures!

HUNTING ON A BUDGET

Hunting an elk without help from an outfitter can be the biggest physical challenge you'll ever make, especially if you're doing it on foot without horses. Moose are bigger, but many tend to be taken reasonably close to a road. Goats and sheep live in remote high country, but you'll probably use horses during your hunt. Day in and day out, an elk hunt in typical mountain country will undoubtedly forge plenty of memories, perhaps not all of them good. Because there's so much public land in elk country with thousands of miles of roads, a do-it-yourself elk hunt is not only feasible, but also quite popular.

Having said that, it's also true that there are probably more hunters who hire outfitters to take them hunting for elk than for any other big game species. Elk country being what it is, most people don't have the equipment or logistical means to get close to the quarry. Compounding the problem is the necessity of getting the large animal out of the woods.

On the other hand, plenty of hunters opt to go it alone, to do it their way rather thAn depending on someone else. This isn't necessarily stubbornness or pride, though it might indeed include both of those human traits, but also a monetary consideration. Many folks just don't have the money to plunk down on an outfitted elk hunt. Instead, they pool their resources, budget their trip, and hunt on public land.

Camp may consist of tents, or some type of pickup camper

or travel trailer. In some areas where elk are handy to roads, an inexpensive motel may serve as the hunt base. Be aware, however, that in small towns close to good elk country, you might have a problem finding a room. Book one far enough in advance so you don't have to buy an unwanted tent or sleep in your pickup truck.

A four-wheel drive pickup is the standard choice of vehicle, and more and more hunters are showing up with ATVs as well. Experienced hunters will shun motorized travel and penetrate the woods afoot, using vehicles only to get them to where they'll hike in from a road. Some hunters will be content to roar around in machines, taking cursory walks here and there. Though ATVs may come in handy in some areas to retrieve animals—where legal— they will most likely be used within the ranks of those elk hunters who go home empty-handed.

The need to get an elk carcass to a road is nicely solved, however, when all members of the party pitch in and lug their share of the load. In some cases, it's possible to hire a packer to perform this chore, but teamwork among the group is usually the primary method of accomplishing this necessary task.

Obviously, much planning and homework need to be done before heading to elk country. The seemingly simple necessity of getting a nonresident tag may prove to be a nightmare in states that require lottery draws. Of course, the where-to-go aspect looms as the major

Obviously, much planning and homework need to be done before heading to elk country.

obstacle, especially during general seasons when the woods are full of hunters and elk are at their elusive best.

Despite these problems, a do-it-yourself elk hunt is immensely satisfactory to folks who enjoy the challenge of being independent and self-reliant. The vast majority of elk hunters take matters into their own hands, and would have it no other way.

My elk hunts were do-it-yourself affairs for the first 15 years I hunted the big animals of the West. One of my early hunts was in Colorado where I was joined by a couple of relatives who knew nothing about elk hunting. The three of us were absolute novices, but at least we knew some folks who would start us off in the right direction. They drew a rough map and told us where to go; from then on we were on our own.

No one got an elk on that trip, but it was a learning experience. It was on that hunt that I was determined to really study elk and elk hunting. I realized how much I didn't know about them, and sought all the information I could find. That was in the days before videos and TV hunting shows, so I turned to the few books on the matter, and began seeking advice from veteran elk hunters. My school would be in the woods, and I had a long uphill battle ahead.

For the first several years I hunted elk on public lands in Utah with a few pals who knew as much about elk hunting as I did—not much. We weren't in

This hunter appears to be in the backcountry, but he's only a half mile from a road on public land. Much elk country is easily accessible.

tight with any ranchers whose land produced the best elk hunting, so we hunted with the crowds on BLM land that offered so-so hunting.

I'd also make journeys to nearby Colorado and hunt in national forests. Crowding by other hunters was even worse, and I learned early on what it was like to compete intensely for an elk. I'd never seen anything like it, even in the East when hunting whitetails. You might say I cut my teeth with hordes of hunters in the elk woods. There's an old saying that the flash of so much hunter orange in the woods can easily blind you.

Since those days I've hunted with many outfitters on fully guided hunts as well as drop camps. I've also maintained an unswerving interest in hunting on my own with the rest of the public. If I had the option of hunting guided or unguided, I'd opt for the latter every time. Though I count many outfitters and guides as close personal friends, I'd much rather make my own decisions in the elk woods. If I want to turn left instead of right, or go to one mountain instead of another, I can do that when I'm hunting solo. I worked for 15 years as a forest ranger and wildlife biologist, and have always considered the woods to be a comfortable place to be in. Perhaps it's pride as well as personal preference that attracts me to hunting without being guided.

There are some very important reasons why hunting solo for elk can be a bad idea. The primary reason is safety. The nature of elk country is perilous, given the broken, steep terrain cluttered with deadfalls, rocky slopes, timber, and underbrush. If an accident happens when a person is hunting alone, the consequences could be severe.

Besides the safety factor, it's no fun if you kill an elk and must pack it out by yourself if it's not within reach of a vehicle. Then again, some folks view that ordeal as the ultimate challenge and welcome it. Of course, it's always best to have a companion along, preferably one who has a strong back and isn't given to easy hernias.

Some of my fondest elk hunting memories recall trips I used to take in Wyoming before I moved there. I'd drive to the end of a road, park my pickup, and climb up a mountain with enough gear on my back to keep me going for four or five days. To me this was elk hunting at its best. I was a free spirit, pitching my tent where and when I wanted to, and roaming the huge country with no specific objective in mind. I was a mountain vagabond, catching trout or shooting a grouse to augment my meals, and following no one's directions.

By taking your own camp, whether it's an RV or tent, you can save money by camping on public land.

I shot a four-by-five bull on one of those trips. He fell on a steep hillside and slid to the very bottom of a canyon. By the time I got to him, shooting light was over and darkness was fast approaching. I cleared a spot for a campfire and soon had a cheery blaze going. The temperature dropped swiftly when the sun disappeared, and it was nearing midnight when I was done. The bull was gutted, skinned, and most of the carcass was boned. I'd finish the job in the morning.

I washed my hands in a tiny brook, laid my sleeping bag on some soft fir boughs, and prepared a late-night snack. I rinsed and sliced up part of the elk's heart and cooked it up with onion and pepper in my small aluminum skillet. After washing it down with steaming hot coffee, I laid back on my bag, watching the flames of the small fire reflect off the bark of nearby trees. I was bone tired, and sleep would come easily.

In the morning I completed the boning chore and had the first load ready to go shortly after sunrise. It took several trips to pack out the meat, and I was ready for the last one just before dark. On my last trip I met an outfitter and his client on the trail. They looked me over

with a flashlight and offered to help, but I declined. Somehow I wanted to finish the whole process by myself. As one of Frank Sinatra's popular songs went: "I did it my way." Indeed I did, and that elk offers some of my fondest memories. It seems the hunts that cause the most pain are the ones that stay with you the longest.

Many years have passed since that hunt. I still hunt alone, but I do so with more care and take just a bit more time to do things that were more quickly done years ago. The challenge is still there, and always will be, as long as elk are roaming our forests. And, thanks to good wildlife practices and people who care, that appears to be a permanent situation. Whether you hunt by yourself or with pals, a do-it-yourself elk hunt, in my viewpoint, is the quintessential form of hunting. And you don't need to squeeze the trigger to go home with a smile on your face. It's always a

bonus when that happens, especially when you're with family members or close companions who can share those memories with you.

HUNTING ELK ON **YOUR OWN**

Each year at my elk hunting seminars, I talk to people who would love to hunt elk but say they can't afford it. They believe that the long trip to elk country is too expensive for their means, and an elk hunt remains an elusive fantasy. That's a shame, because you can easily make a hunt very affordable. With careful planning and a willingness to be thrifty, you can indeed make a hunt that won't ravage your bank account. Would you believe that you could do it for less than $750?

The nice thing about hunting on your own is the opportunity to make your own decisions, such as taking a nap after a grueling hike.

Let's assume you live 2,000 miles from Colorado, where you intend to hunt. I'm selecting Colorado as an example because it's the only major elk state where nonresidents can buy an elk tag across the counter. Other states require a lottery draw or first-come, first-served system. Colorado's nonresident elk tag is also among the cheapest in the West ($450), and the state also has more national forests (11, with more than 14 million acres of public land) than any other in elk country. If you intend to hunt another state, you may have to pay more for an elk tag.

First, you should choose your companions carefully. Nothing can ruin a trip quicker than a member of the group who doesn't fit in. Each hunter should have the same expectations, and be willing to abide by a frugal budget as well as minor discomforts caused by your economy plan. Considering ideal space limitations, three hunters are optimum. This number works best when driving to and from your hunt, and when camping. Let's say you're going hunting with George and Jack.

Once you've determined who your companions will be, you need to decide whose vehicle you'll use. In my opinion, a four-wheel drive is a must in elk country, and it should be equipped with a sturdy jack, four tire chains, jumper cables, tow chain, and other routine gear. We'll assume that one of you has such a rig and is willing to put several thousand miles on it.

To meet your budget, you'll need to camp and hunt on public land. A small camp cost may be incurred if you camp in a U.S. Forest Service designated campground, but many are available for free during hunting season. In most national forests you can merely camp at no charge in a place that strikes your fancy. Be sure you know the rules, and buy a map of the forest you're hunting in (around $3). Choose a camp shelter you already own, but be aware that in elk country you can always expect extremely cold weather. Most hunters own some sort of camp rig, whether it's a tent, camp trailer, pickup cab-over camper, van, motor home, etc. In the case of the latter, consider towing a hunting vehicle, but remember that the cost of fuel for a motor home can be considerably higher than that for a pickup or sport utility vehicle.

Sit down with your buddies at a planning session before your trip and determine who can provide essential camping gear, such as cookstoves, lanterns, axes, utensils, first-aid kit, and other necessary items. Most hunters already own such equipment. To transport an elk out of the woods, you'll also need sturdy backpacks, a sharp saw and knife, rope, meat sacks, etc. You may need to spend a few dollars to buy items such as extra lantern mantles, propane, lantern fuel, etc. You'll also need items such as toilet paper, paper towels, paper plates, plastic utensils, and dishwashing soap. You can save money by using real plates and silverware, but you'll obviously need

Nothing can ruin a trip quicker than a member of the group who doesn't fit in.

This Montana camp was set up by several hunters who drove from the East Coast. They hunted on public land and beat the cost of an outfitted hunt.

to wash them. Let's say you'll spend $75 for paper goods and camp supplies, at a shared cost of $25 each.

When considering food, we're going to assume that it's not an extra expense. Look at it this way: wherever you are, you must eat, whether you're hunting, at home, or on the job. If you'll purchase your food when it's on sale before the hunt and store or freeze it, you'll save plenty of money. For example, I buy chicken leg quarters on sale at $.49 or less per pound, and cook and freeze them. I also cook chili, stew, lasagna, and other foods that are easily frozen, using venison from the freezer to cut down on the expense of buying meat. In fact, I use wild game exclusively. Granted, it's not free when you consider the cost of hunting, but it's not added to your elk-hunting budget. I freeze those meals until I'm ready to hunt, and keep the frozen food in coolers and thaw it as required. All you need to do is heat it when you come in from hunting. Before your planning session, snoop around your pantry and grab some canned or packaged foods that you can pool together. You'll likely find

some dusty cans of soup and vegetables that need to be eaten soon.

On your trip to elk country, take turns driving. One person should stay awake with the driver to keep him company. Lodging should not be part of your trip cost. If everyone is sleepy, pull over in a highway rest area for several hours. If you really want a bed to stretch out in and a shower, rent an inexpensive motel room. You should

As they say, "The fun of the hunt is over when you squeeze the trigger." That's when the work begins and you must transport your elk from the woods to a road.

be able to rent a room with two beds and bring in a rollaway bed for under $50. You'll likely be driving on Interstate highways most of the way, and the current legal speed limit of 70 mph on most roads allows you to zing right along.

Gasoline for your rig will be a major expense. Let's say you drive 2,000 miles each way and another 500 miles while hunting. That's 4,500 miles. Figuring your vehicle gets 12 miles per gallon, you'll buy 375 gallons of gasoline at an average of $1.30 per gallon, for a total of about $488. Split three ways, that's around $163 each. Add another $10 each for motor oil, coolant, and windshield wiper fluid.

Meals on the road should be planned with your budget in mind. For breakfast I have coffee, juice, and a pastry. I bring along a cooler with assorted cold cuts and condiments to make sandwiches for lunch, and for dinner I look for a place with a big salad bar that goes with the meal. Instead of a T-bone I eat a chicken-fried steak, a pop, or coffee for a total cost of around $8 to $9.

Of course, the person who owns the vehicle will accrue "wear and tear" expenses. Tires and parts wear down, and the extra mileage decreases the vehicle's value. Let's make this less complicated and work it this way. Say George uses his vehicle for the elk hunt. For the rest of the year on other hunting and/or fishing trips, you and Jack will use your vehicles. It doesn't take a lot of trips for avid outdoorsmen to drive plenty of miles, even fairly close to home. The next time you make a long-distance trip, another per-

son should do the driving. Before you leave on the trip, everyone should put $100 in a kitty. A designated banker holds the money. All trip costs, except for personal items such as medicine, toiletries, and gifts, should come from the bank. When the bank is getting low, everyone tosses in another equal amount. In this way, you don't need to keep complicated records on who paid for gasoline last, or meals, and how much.

If you'll follow these suggestions, here's what your approximate cost per person will amount to: Elk tag: $450; camp supplies: $25; and gasoline and vehicle costs: $173, for a total of $648. Remember, a bare-bones hunt might require some extra sacrifice, but this plan works. Besides doing it myself, I know several hunters who save plenty of money each year. Indeed, an elk hunt could be easily within your reach. Now you have no excuse. Plan that hunt today!

You may not have anyone to help if you get in trouble except for your hunting buddies. Don't try to drive to places that might get your vehicle stuck.

OUTFITTERS

These hunters each took an elk by booking a trip with a reputable Montana outfitter.

THE OUTFITTED HUNT

Since elk hunting is a downright tough activity, some form of help is always appreciated, if not necessary in some cases. Because of the possible hardships, an outfitter would seem to be the perfect answer but there are drawbacks, some obvious, some not so obvious.

Cost is a primary consideration. You'll be looking at $2,500 to $10,000 or more, with an average at about $4,000. Hunts can last for five, seven, or ten days but generally no longer hunts are offered these days. Be aware that the outfitter will be likely to have two prices for each hunt, depending on whether it's a one-on-one or two-on-one. A one-on-one means one guide per hunter; two-on-one means one guide for two hunters. Obviously, the one-on-one will be more expen-

An outfitter takes care of the logistical problem of getting your gear into a backcountry camp.

This hunter and her guide teamed up to find this Colorado bull. The guide knew the country and placed the hunter in a location where elk crossed an opening in the forest.

sive, typically running $4,000 or more. If the cost seems too high, and you live some distance from elk country, consider this point if you make frequent trips with your buddies and have been largely unsuccessful. How much money have you spent on those trips without getting an elk? It's quite possible that one outfitted hunt could actually be cheaper if you are focused on finally getting a decent animal.

Two factors come into play here. First is the assumption that getting an elk is mandatory to make your western journey a success. The other is the assumption that the outfitter can guarantee you an elk. The latter is, unfortunately, never the case, with one notable exception—the outfitter is hunting within a high fence. No matter how good a fair chase outfitter's area is, he can't absolutely guarantee you an elk. Too many things can go wrong – the weather, elk behavior, your ability to get to where the elk are (since strenuous hiking may be required), and your skills as a hunter. The high fence operator, on the other hand, has a herd of domestic animals that typically are easily approached. In most scenarios, your hunt is over in a half day, you have no aches or sore muscles, and you hardly have dirt on your boots. You need no hunting license, since the animals are privately owned; there are no seasons and you can shoot all the elk you want (as long as you can afford the premium cost of buying them). You also cannot enter such an animal in the Boone & Crockett Club awards program, because high fence hunting violates of the B&C's rules of fair chase.

I know some of the top outfitters in the West. As good as they are, some of their hunters go home empty-handed. Too many variables can affect the outcome of a hunt. So how do you find a reputable outfitter? Are there some sure-fire methods? Yes, there are good methods, but again, all you can do is sort out the good guys from the bad guys, knowing the good guys can't always produce. The sad truth is that there are a number of swindlers who pose as legitimate outfitters. You won't know you've been had until the hunt is over.

I can recall a few nightmare hunts that I wish I could forget. One involved an outfitter who promised a horseback trip

Don't be surprised if you make a long-lasting friendship with your guide or outfitter.

in the backcountry. I was with a party of five hunters, one of whom had arranged the trip through a friend. The trip was full of surprises. Instead of a backcountry camp, we were treated to a spot that was not only accessible by Cadillacs, but was smack under a major utility line corridor with wires that sizzled all day and night. The outfitter had never been there in his life, and had no horses. He hired a wrangler to bring in horses, but the wrangler had never been in that area, either.

We learned the outfitter was terrified of horses, and knew little about elk hunting. He insisted we leave camp when the sun was fully up, and didn't have a clue about elk habits and behavior. None of us got an elk, and it was simply an awful hunt. Since I was the guest of someone else, I didn't say much, but I was as disappointed as the other men in our group. None of them had ever killed an elk before and had been eagerly looking forward to the trip. This was the worst ever of my hunts, and I'm glad to say there have been no others quite like that one.

Other complaints I've heard include hunts where there were far more hunters in camp than indicated when the hunt was booked, having too many hunters per guide, camps located in areas where there were few, if any, elk, camps with guides who were either inexperienced or were brand-new to the area, camps with lazy guides, and on and on.

So how do you measure an outfitter? Are there any reliable ways to check him out? Several options exist. Magazine ads are a primary way for outfitters to spotlight their business. If you respond to an ad, an outfitter will likely send you a brochure and perhaps a reference list. Be aware that he's only going to send you names of hunters who were happy campers.

When you call the reference, ask him to provide you with the names of other hunters in camp, since people often trade business cards. Find out all you can about the operation—details that the outfitter might not tell you. For example, how far from camp do you hunt? Do you hike there or ride a horse? Even if you ride a horse, some foot hunting will be necessary—what can you expect? How many elk were seen, and how many were taken? What size?

An important question that you should ask the outfitter, and one that he won't want to hear, is his average hunter success rate. I would side with the outfitter on this, because the question isn't fair. Here's an example. I was on a wilderness hunt with four other hunters. It was prime time during the peak of the rut, and elk were bugling. When the hunt ended another hunter and I had each taken a nice six-by-six bull. Hunter number three

shot at two good bulls and missed both. Hunter number four had his sights set on a 350 B&C bull, and passed on three bulls, all around the 300 mark. Hunter number five simply couldn't see elk and get on them quickly enough to shoot. He had two opportunities on bulls less than 200 yards away in sparse timber but never took a shot. The hunter success rate on that hunt was 40 percent, but it should have been 100 percent if everyone had cashed in on their opportunities.

Don't expect an outfitted hunt to be easy. That's a common mistake, because people often believe that just because you have a guide, he'll be able to quickly find you an elk with a minimum of effort. Some of my toughest hunts have been with a guide. I can recall hiking over treacherous terrain in severe weather conditions for days at a time.

Remember, too, that a guide will invariably be young, full of pep, and capable of practically running around in the mountains. If you aren't up to his pace, sit down with him and have a little chat. Tell him politely that you're employing him, and that you really don't want to come out of the woods on a stretcher, or worse—in a body bag. Make no mistake, it happens every year.

A guide should never be more than a couple steps in front of you. If he insists in maintaining a considerable distance ahead, tell him to slow it down. Not only will it be easier on you, but also if he jumps an elk or sees one and you aren't there in time to make a shot, he'll be doing you a disservice. If a guide seems

A guide should never be more than a couple steps in front of you.

to be working you harder than you like, it's probably because he doesn't realize you're not in his league. Unless you say something, he won't know. It's fairly common for guides to have a contest with other guides in camp. They'll throw some money in a pool, and the guide whose client gets the biggest bull collects the money. That's even more of an incentive for him to get you into prime country where more physical effort than usual may be required.

Be sure you're on the same page as your outfitter. Be certain the "t's" are crossed and the "i's" are dotted. You don't want any surprises. Find out all the details you need to know before you book. Be sure the outfitter knows what kind of animal you're looking for. Some outfitters may have few, if any, bulls that score 300 B&C, for example.

Your outfitted hunt can be one of the finest hunting memories of your life, or it can be a profound disappointment. The more planning and research you do, the better chance that you'll come home with a smile—whether you get an elk or not.

Drop camps typically offer the best of all worlds. For a reasonable fee, an outfitter packs you and your gear into a camp in prime elk country.

DROP CAMPS

It would seem that a drop camp offers the best of all worlds to a hunter who is unfamiliar with elk country. For a modest price, you're transported into a good area by an outfitter, dropped off at a comfortable camp, and left on your own. When the hunt is over, your outfitter picks you up and hauls you and your game out. Sounds perfect, right? It is indeed, if the outfitter has some integrity in the first place and puts you in a camp where there are some living, breathing elk within a reasonable distance from where you're based.

Why would an outfitter put a camp in a marginal area, or even in a place where there are no elk? After all, that's not only unethical, it's immoral. The reasons are not all that surprising. In the first place, a drop camp doesn't offer much profit, so the outfitter might not be very motivated to go the extra mile, so to speak. He'll be plenty busy with tending details for his regular guided hunts. That brings up the next point. The guided hunters will be based in prime country, and the outfitter obviously doesn't want competition from other hunters. He has no control over other hunters if he's on public land, but he can control his drop camp hunters by locating them far enough away from his main operation. Finally, drop camp hunters are independent and willing to hunt hard on their own. The outfitter shares his territory with strangers, with the risk of those people coming back on their own and offering direct competition in the future. For all those reasons, too many drop camps are placed in areas where they shouldn't be.

How can you find out if your drop

In some instances, a cabin may be your shelter in a drop camp.

In most drop camps, a tent will be your home. It will probably be supplied with a wood stove, cooking stove, lantern, and cots.

camp is in a good spot? The ideal way would be to ask the outfitter to tell you where it is, and then inquire with the wildlife agency as to its potential. The problem here is the outfitter's obvious reluctance to divulge his spots. He may believe you'll be using him to gain information for yourself with no notion of booking with him. Once you've booked the hunt, however, the outfitter may be willing to provide you with maps or at least tell you what maps to order. The bottom line is that drop camps might be one of the worst hunts you've ever experienced. On the other hand, it might be one of the best.

Even if there are elk around, you might have some difficulty locating them. You'll be in unfamiliar country, but if the outfitter has put you in an area with a reasonable number of elk, you should have a decent chance of scoring if you're a good hunter. The outfitter or guide who packs you into camp should be able to provide you with general information, if not specific tips on places to hunt. When you arrive at the place the outfitter meets

you, ask if he can point out spots on a map. Most will be willing to do that. Be sure to ask him the legal boundaries of the area you're hunting. For example, you might be camped on public land close to a ranch that's off-limits to hunting. If there are no posted signs, an unmarked fence might be your only guideline. In some places there may be no fences at all.

When you plan your drop camp hunt, be sure to ask the outfitter what supplies he'll be providing. And do yourself a favor. Anticipate that some essential items may be broken or missing and bring them yourself. A missing or broken mantle for your lantern may leave you literally in the dark, and a low supply of fuel for the lantern may also be a serious problem. The same is true for your cookstove. Best yet, bring your own lantern, two-burner stove, and fuel. You can adapt to some minor things that go wrong, but if you don't have light, heat, and a means to cook, you'll be most unhappy.

Outfitters offer different drop

camp options. In some, you provide all the food. In others, the outfitter provides the food and may even make available a wrangler to tend horses. Most camps will have a tent to sleep in and a cook tent, or one tent may be used for sleeping and cooking. The tent may or may not have cots. Find out in advance if they do so you can bring portable cots or air mattresses. Obviously, the cheapest hunts will be those that are bare bones and have no frills.

Be sure you find out before you book if the outfitter will require you to pack your elk to camp, or if he will pick up the animals where they fell. That's a big consideration, because you'll need to transport several hundred pounds of meat over rough terrain if you're on your own. Bring your own meat bags to store quarters, whether you hang them in the field or at camp. Drop camps can be an economical way to hunt elk. Pick your companions carefully and plan thoroughly—you don't want any surprises, particularly unpleasant ones.

Outfitters may offer several options. They may drop you off and check on you once or twice, or leave a wrangler and some horses with you.

FIREARMS

The author with his latest favorite rifle for elk: a
Remington .300 short-action Ultra Mag.

The author with his Winchester Model 70 in .30/06 caliber. He has taken almost two dozen elk with this rifle.

TOP ELK RIFLES

- Browning A-Bolt
- Remington Model 7
- Remington 700
- Remington .300 short-action UltraMag.
- Weatherby .300 Mag.
- Winchester Model 70, .30/06 Featherweight
- Winchester Model 70, .270 caliber
- Winchester-Browning WSM (Winchester short action)

TOP ELK LOADS

- .270
- 7mm Remington Mag.
- .30/06
- .300 Win Mag.
- .338 Win Mag.
- Remington .300 Ultra Mag.

AN ELK is not only big, he's tenacious, which means he doesn't give up easily. He also lives in heavily timbered mountain ranges, and routinely feeds in open grassy meadows where a long shot might be mandatory. Put those elements together, and you have an interesting item of discussion among veteran and first-time hunters.

Because I write a great deal about elk, and have been hunting them most of my adult life, many readers ask if one rifle is by far and away the best. Is there truly a perfect firearm for elk? One that's head and shoulders above the rest?

In a nutshell—no. That's like asking if there's a perfect pickup truck, or a perfect washing machine. Each gets the job done, and it really comes down to a matter of loyalty, but each must be matched for the task that must be performed. A two-wheel drive lightweight pickup truck is no match for truly nasty terrain, but a four-wheel drive heavy-duty rig will nicely get the job done. In easy country and on dry roads the smaller pickup gets around easily—but don't make demands on it when the going gets tough.

That's the way it is with firearms. You can kill an elk with a .22 if the conditions are perfect, but don't count on that little rifle when the chips are down. That's why I tell hunters who ask about firearms that the rifle they use on white-tails in Wisconsin, Pennsylvania, and Texas is fine for elk—maybe. There are, in my opinion, some concerns that must be addressed.

Jack O'Connor, the legendary shooting writer who championed the .270 for elk and most other North American big game animals (grizzlies and brown bears were an exception), believed that bullet placement was the bottom line. Put the bullet in the boiler room, advocated O'Connor, and the elk was yours. O'Connor's logic was not original. Anyone who hunts will tell you that bullet placement is the key to success, but O'Connor made this his mantra. And, using his logic, a .270 will indeed put down any bull elk on the planet. But, let's make the wild assumption that just maybe you don't have the perfect shot, and your bullet has trouble getting into the boiler room. What then? Is the .270 still the caliber of choice?

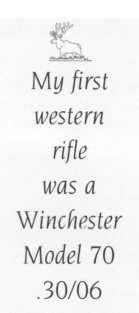

My first western rifle was a Winchester Model 70 .30/06

My first western rifle was a Winchester Model 70 .30/06. It was a featherweight, topped with a Weaver four-power scope, and I bought it only because there wasn't a pre-64 .270 in the store. It was 1964 when I made the purchase, and Winchester was in the process of eliminating the pre-64 version. I wasn't interested in the new, untried Model 70, and opted for the pre-64 30/06, though I was a bit disappointed. After all, I was an O'Connor groupie,

and the .270 had been my fantasy gun for years. As it turned out, the .30/06 exceeded my highest expectations. I went on to take 19 elk with that rifle, and never lost an animal. I can't say that I didn't miss any, but fortunately, I never hit one that I wasn't able to recover.

A close call occurred on a hunt in British Columbia. I had called in a bull with a cow call, and had only one very long opportunity across a basin. I thought I hit the bull on the third shot, and made a tedious, grueling search. My guide and I actually gave up and decided the bull wasn't hit. We left the area, headed back to camp, when I suddenly had a strange sense of recall. In my mind I saw the bull lurch at the shot, and I heard a heavy thud in the forest a few seconds after it disappeared in the timber.

My guide thought I was crazy when I told him the bull was dead, and I ran back down to the spot we'd already searched. It was a bizarre scenario, and I wasn't at all surprised to find the bull, lying on his belly in a small stand of spruce saplings. The branches had closed over him, with only the tips of his antlers protruding. I shuddered when I realized how close I'd come to losing him. While searching, I had passed within mere feet of the dead bull.

General Chuck Yeager, who was a member of our hunting party, heard me shoot, and accompanied my guide and me to pack the meat out later in the afternoon. Chuck joked about me requiring three shots to down the bull, and later that evening presented me with his .300 Weatherby, but only if I'd retire my Winchester. He didn't know I already planned on giving it to my son, Dan, so it was a win-win all the way around.

I used the Weatherby on several hunts, and later became enamored with the 7mm Rem Mag. I acquired a Browning A-Bolt, and was pleased with its performance, taking a dozen elk with it. This rifle was superb at long-range shooting, and I wasn't at all hesitant about reaching out to a bull that was 350 yards distant.

Over the years, I've been in the company of hundreds of hunters in camps around the West, and I've seen some interesting situations with elk and firearms. In every case, without exception, poor bullet placement was the cause of missing or wounding an animal, whether it was due to a long shot that the gun was incapable of making, or a shot that struck in a nonvital area. I know a veteran outfitter who carries a .243 on elk hunts. Too light? Absolutely, but in the hands of this man, who shoots only if he has a perfect shot, it's deadly. However, I would never recommend the .243 for elk. I consider the .270 the minimum caliber.

We must realize that hunting is not a perfect sport. We often don't have the luxury of time when we make our shot, and the environment in which we hunt in may not be user-friendly. Weather may be a critical issue, as well as the negative aspects of steep, rough terrain, high altitudes, and heavy timber. We might not have a steady rifle rest, the elk might be moving or partially

Firearms are always topics of discussion. Two hunters compare notes.

obscured by vegetation we might be breathing hard and we might suffer a case of "elk fever" in which our brain goes to pieces at the sight of the quarry. All these elements can combine to work against the accurate shot we hope to make.

For all these reasons, I'm a firm believer that bigger is better (but not too big) when it comes to elk rifles, though I don't advocate using a gun that you'd take on an elephant or Cape buffalo hunt. You can leave the .375 H&H or .416 Rigby at home. Having said that, I'd be comfortable with practically any medium to big bore, such as the .30/06, 7mm Rem Mag, 300 Win Mag, .338 Win Mag, or any of the Weatherby Mags.

Lately I've been enamored with new Remington offerings, notably the .300 Ultra Mag and the .300 short-action Ultra Mag. The latter claimed my last two elk, and I have a growing fondness for it. It weighs in at six and one-eighth pounds—slightly over seven pounds with scope, sling, and ammo. This firearm

Todd Smith, editor-in-chief of Outdoor Life magazine, took this bull with a favorite and popular rifle, a Remington Model 700 in 7mm Rem Mag caliber.

has been on the market for three years, and I've claimed a number of big game animals with it other than elk, such as moose, deer, antelope, caribou, and black bears. I've never seen the quarry hit the ground so decisively as when touched by a bullet from that gun.

Proper bullets for elk are also a great subject for debate. My preferences are 165- and 180-grain bullets, and I've never had a profound affinity for any particular type. I've had the experience of killing elk with Nosler Partitions, Winchester Silvertips, Federal Trophy Bonded Bear Claws, and Remington Core-Lokts, with the latter accounting for most of my elk. In a nutshell, these bullets have been used for years and have been thoroughly tested around the world. They've held up to the challenges offered them, and I wouldn't have a problem using any of those four types on any elk hunt.

Practically every article on firearms evaluates different calibers according to ballistics. While bullet velocity and ener-gy is extremely important, it matters not one whit if a bullet is traveling at 2,800 feet per second or 2,700 feet per second, or if it delivers 1,400 foot pounds of ener-gy or 1,550 foot-pounds. Many gun afi-cionados will argue that point, and some gun writers will write thousands of words attempting to make a point for a particu-lar rifle, saying it's the last word for elk, but I make my claim based on personal observations. Your gun is only as good as your capability of making an accurate shot. An elk hit in the guts with a .270 is wounded just as badly as an elk struck in the guts with a .300 Win Mag. The result with either is the same—you have a badly wounded animal on your hands that you might not recover.

It's far better to use a firearm that you have confidence in—and not one that you are reluctant to shoot because it kicks like the devil or makes so much noise that it unnerves you. Why own a gun that you have little confidence in? Why not hunt with one that you're com-

fortable with? There are ways to alter a firearm and protect yourself so that recoil and noise are no longer irritating or crippling factors.

Recoil can be eliminated by two basic techniques. Get a good recoil pad such as the amazing R-3 that currently fits only synthetic Remington stocks. However, this technology will undoubtedly be made available for other brands and stock types as well. A muzzlebrake will also eliminate recoil dramatically, but increases noise. Resolve the noise factor by wearing one of the ear protective devices on the market today.

Let's look at what makes a good elk rifle and eliminate the statistics about ballistics, if we can agree that a rifle needs to be flat shooting and will deliver the bullet to the target area with enough foot-pounds of energy to quickly dispatch an elk.

Quality doesn't have to be a fac-

tor. You can have one of the best custom rifles in the world, such as a .300 Jarrett, which will cost you around $6,000, and still miss every elk you shoot at if you don't know how to shoot, or you shoot when you shouldn't have. The Jarrett will punch holes in a distant target with a tiny group that will astound most observers, but remember that the vitals on an elk are around 20 inches by 15 inches.

By all means, buy the Jarrett if you want incredible accuracy, but learn how to shoot well enough to give that gun the respect it's due. If you can't afford the Jarrett, you might want to consider the Remington 710 in .30/06 caliber, for example, that will cost you about $400 including scope. This firearm will not group bullets like a more expensive custom rifle, but it's plenty adequate for elk.

Don't bring a rifle with poor ballistics on an elk hunt and expect it to reach out at 300 yards, unless you've practiced intensely with it at that distance. I'm referring to calibers such as the beloved .30-30 Winchester, the .35 Remington, and the .444 Marlin. These are admittedly short-range guns and will kill an elk, but they simply aren't capable of shooting long distances, since gravity does terrible things to the comparatively low-velocity bullets.

Put some thought into the weight of your rifle, because you'll probably be carrying it over your shoulder, perhaps across awful terrain. I like a gun that weighs in at seven pounds or so, including sling, scope, and a full clip of ammo. Synthetic stocks and other high-tech improvements have allowed gun-makers to produce rifles that are far lighter today than they were a couple of decades ago.

Your gun's action is a matter of personal preference. The majority of elk hunters use a bolt action because it's strong, dependable, easy to clean, and easy to operate. It's also easy to remove, so you can clean the gun readily, as well as to demonstrate to an airline clerk that your rifle is inoperable when the bolt is out. Some hunters like a pump action, which is also dependable, as is the carbine. But I'm not at all a fan of a semi-automatic rifle. I've seen too many instances where a semi-auto jammed when the hunter was shooting at an elk, or trying to shoot. The semi-auto also gives a false sense of confidence. Some hunters take the first shot too quickly, knowing that they have several more quick shots to follow. Unfortunately, the first shot will usually be your best opportunity. Make it count.

A scope is mandatory in my opinion —no other discussion necessary. See the chapter on optics for information on scopes. A sling is also required, since you'll undoubtedly do some hiking. I like a wide, single sling that fits comfortably on my shoulder. There are other types of slings that fit over both shoulders, and some allow you to carry your firearm at different positions.

Practice at different yardages. Here's the standard scenario before elk season:

A scope is mandatory in my opinion— no other discussion necessary.

the average hunter—we'll call him Sam —goes to the range and puts up a target at 100 yards. Sam sets up the rifle on a sturdy, comfortable bench rest, and fires three shots. If the group is tight and where it needs to be, Sam smiles, puts the gun away, and can't wait for opening morning. Life is good.

Now it's elk season and our hunter spots a bull across a canyon at 352 yards. He knows it's 352 yards because he's confirmed the distance with his rangefinder. Unfortunately, Sam has no clue where his bullets are hitting at 352 yards because he's never shot at that distance. He has a vague idea of the ballistics of his rifle and ammo, but isn't sure precisely where to hold. In fact, the majority of hunters fall into Sam's category.

The correct thing to do is to shoot at different yardages up to the distance you feel comfortable with, so you'll know how your rifle performs. To eliminate the need to remember bullet drop at different yardages, write up a small chart and tape it to the stock of your rifle so you'll have a quick and easy reference.

Always use a rest of some sort if you make a long shot. If you can't draw a steady bead, no rifle in the world will make an accurate shot. Use a handy rock, log, tree, fence post, or whatever, or use a bipod or one of the shooting sticks such as the Stoney Point or Underwood. A rifle may make or break your hunt. Understand it and use it. You won't be sorry when the moment of truth arrives and your elk offers a shot.

MUZZLELOADING

The author and Tony Knight (right), inventor of the in-line muzzleloader, teamed up to take this bull with .50 caliber muzzleloading rifles.

The author hunts on a wet, dreary day. Moisture is always a problem with muzzleloaders. If the powder is wet or damp, it won't ignite.

LIKE ARCHERY equipment and modern firearms, muzzleloading has also undergone a profound evolution over the years. If Davy Crockett and Daniel Boone could see what's happened to black powder guns, they wouldn't believe their eyes. But despite the new technology, these guns must still be loaded at the muzzle, and the hunter gets only one shot—then he or she must repeat the reloading process.

Several states have special muzzleloading seasons, which gives the guns a practical value. The special seasons not only help distribute hunter pressure and ease crowding in the woods, but some are held during the rut, as well as late in the fall, giving hunters an advantage in locating elk. While these seasons are held in high regard, there are plenty of hunters who simply like the aspect and challenges of hunting with a muzzleloader.

I recall muzzleloader hunts for elk in Washington and New Mexico during special seasons that offered hunting opportunities in areas with big bulls and few hunters. I never felt undergunned with the firearms even though they don't have the ballistic qualities of center-fire rifles.

There are basically two types of muzzleloaders: the flint-lock and percussion. The former is the most primitive, requir-

Practice is essential in becoming familiar with a muzzleloader, not only to sight it in but to practice loading smoothly.

ing the shooter to not only charge the barrel from the muzzle end, but to also apply powder externally. Here's how it works. A small amount of powder is applied on a pan, and when the trigger is activated, a flint hammer falls and strikes steel, creating a spark. The spark ignites the powder on the pan, creating a small explosion, which transmits heat through the flash hole. The heat ignites the powder in the barrel that is behind the projectile, causing a much larger explosion, thereby propelling the projectile forward and out of the barrel.

The percussion firearm uses an explosive cap that fits on a nipple, eliminating the external pan, flint hammer, and steel. The cap contains a fulminate of mercury, used for the express purpose of muzzleloading firearms. Today, some models use a 209 primer which was originally used only for shotgun shells. When the hammer on a percussion gun is activated, it strikes the cap or primer that explodes, sending heat into the flash hole and igniting the powder behind the projectile. It becomes immediately apparent that the percussion

type offers more reliability in very wet weather, because the powder in a flintlock's pan can become moist. If that happens, the powder may not ignite, and there goes the elk of your dreams. Moisture is always an enemy in any type of muzzleloading rifle, because wet powder behind the projectile can also cause a misfire. It's difficult for moisture to reach the powder once it's behind the projectile, but it can get wet simply from the high humidity when it's being carried, or it can become moist when the gun is being loaded.

Muzzleloader firearms are often called "blackpowder rifles," which is technically incorrect when other types of powder are used. Black powder in itself is extremely explosive and unstable, and fouls a barrel to the point where frequent cleaning is required. Many hunters nowadays use Pyrodex as a substitute. It's safer, since it's more stable, and cleaner, though the barrel still needs to be cleaned. Black powder comes in several grades, Fg, FFg, FFFg, and FFFFg. The latter is the finest and is used in flintlock pans, since a quick explosion is necessary. Fg is typically used in shotguns, while FFg and FFFg are used to propel the projectile in the barrel of most rifles. Most elk hunters prefer FFg. Pyrodex comes in different grades, with RS grade used almost exclusively by elk hunters.

To load the firearm, a measured amount of powder is poured into the barrel. The powder can be premeasured and stored in a plastic cylinder, often called a speed-loader. When it's time to load, the cylinder is quickly opened and the powder is dumped into the barrel. Some hunters prefer to carry powder in a horn or other container, pour it into a brass or other type of cylindrical con-

The author's son, Dan, with a good bull he took with a muzzleloader in a special muzzleloader-only unit in New Mexico.

tainer where it can be quickly measured, and then dumped into the barrel. Obviously, the speed-loader saves several seconds, because the powder is already measured and ready to be poured into the barrel. Nevertheless, there are plenty of hunters who prefer the "old-fashioned" process, which is the reason why the flintlock is championed by many folks who are traditionalists and disinterested in any other type of muzzleloader.

About 20 years ago, Tony Knight invented the "in-line" muzzleloader which dramatically changed the sport. Whereas the standard percussion gun has a hammer that's off to the side, the in-line has the striker, cap, nipple, flash hole, powder, and

projectile in a straight line, therefore improving performance and reliability. Many in-lines use a modern rifle primer held in a plastic disk in the chamber in place of the percussion cap. Knight improved his guns throughout the years, as other companies did, and the 209 primer is used extensively in the top models.

Recently, a new type of powder form was introduced to muzzleloader hunters. Pyrodex is pressed into cylindrical pellets of 50 grains. Rather than dealing with loose powder, the hunter simply pops the pellets into the barrel, and then seats the projectile on top. This has obvious advantages, but one that's seldom mentioned is the ability to load the gun without having to raise it vertically, which is required for loose powder, since gravity sends it to the bottom of the barrel. With pellets, the powder can be loaded if the hunter is in a tight place where foliage or limbs don't allow the gun to be easily raised.

To determine the proper load, practice with different powder charges to see what works best. Most hunters use around 100 grains of either black powder or Pyrodex. In some guns, three 50-grain Pyrodex pellets are used. Always be absolutely sure your firearm will accommodate a particular charge by checking the manufacturer's recommendations.

Projectiles come in three basic types, round ball, conical, and saboted. In terms of accuracy, the round ball has the poorest ballistics. It drops quickly and has comparatively lower foot-pounds of energy. Ballistically, the conical bullet is better, and the sabot, a bullet encased in a plastic cup, is best. Most round balls weigh between 180 and 215 grains, depending on the caliber, and the conical bullet is generally much heavier, ranging from 385 to 425 grains. The sabot is lighter, from 180 to 325 grains.

There are several calibers available to muzzleloader hunters, but the .50 and .54 calibers are the top choices, with the .50 caliber the most popular. Many hunters don't realize that the .54 caliber is only 4/100 of an inch bigger than the .50. In my opinion, nothing smaller than the .50 caliber is recommended for elk.

When a round ball is loaded, it's typi-cally seated on a cloth patch, which may or may not be lubricated. Conical bullets and sabots aren't patched. With the powder loaded, the projectile is inserted into the barrel, and it often needs to receive an initial "push." This is effectively done with a bullet starter, a short rod with a palm protector, which allows you to insert the projectile with a sharp tap from the palm of your hand. Once in, the projectile is driven the rest of the way with the ramrod, which is carried under the barrel.

There may be times when a quick second shot is necessary, requiring the hunter to be fast and efficient when loading. When you practice shooting your gun for accuracy, practice your timing as well. Carry your components where you can get at them quickly, and go through the process several times while timing yourself. The extra seconds can amount to success or failure.

Modern muzzleloaders may be fitted with telescopic sights, a practice that often draws fire from hunters who believe the guns shouldn't be high-tech. Some states agree and don't allow scopes. Be sure you know the regulations when you're planning your elk hunt.

There's also plenty of controversy about the so-called "modern-muzzleloaders," chiefly the in-lines, because they're felt to be ballistically superior to the flintlock and standard percussion rifles. It's unfortunate that there's a divisive attitude among hunters. I believe we ought to hunt with whatever our preferences are, and work together to reinforce our sport.

> *To determine the proper load, practice with different powder charges to see what works best.*

OPTICS

When glassing, search into every shaded nook and cranny instead of making a fast cursory look.

Trying to use binoculars while sitting on a horse (or in a moving vehicle) is never a good idea. Always glass from a stable and comfortable position.

I'LL NEVER forget an incident that occurred while hunting elk some years ago. My buddy and I had been hunting all day, and were absolutely whipped. We hadn't seen a fresh track in the snow, though we hiked for miles. Deciding to take a break and eat a candy bar before making our final hike to the road, we sat under a tree and talked about the lousy hunting.

We were about to leave when my pal raised his binoculars and casually glassed a big sagebrush flat surrounded by heavy evergreen timber. It was lightly snowing, and visibility was poor. I was about ready to leave when my companion made a startling statement. "Elk!" he exclaimed. "A bunch of 'em. Out there in the sage next to the timber."

I jumped up and looked but couldn't see any elk. "I don't see them," said I. "Are you sure?"

"Look through your binoculars," my buddy said. "You can't see them with your naked eye." I raised my glasses, and sure enough, there were a bunch of elk about 600 yards away. They were in the sagebrush, but tough to see since they had a light dusting of snow on their pelts. My pal and I eased into the timber and worked our way to them with the wind in our favor. Twenty minutes later my pal tied his tag to a nice five-point bull, and I shot a fat spike.

The message here is clear. Without the binoculars we wouldn't have seen the elk. My buddy has superb vision and terrific "game" eyes, and if he couldn't see the elk with unaided eyes, then no one could. We would have left the area, blissfully ignorant of the elk that were there to be seen. I once read an interesting article written by a famous outdoor scribe who maintained that binoculars are more important than a firearm. "If you can't see the quarry," he argued, "you can't shoot it."

I believe that binoculars are essential from a safety standpoint, as well as to help spot game. Consider this scenario: you're hunting with a scoped rifle but have no binoculars. Suddenly you see something move in the brush, but you can't tell what it is. You raise your rifle and check out the unidentified object, and realize, to your horror, that you're aiming your firearm at a human being. Avoid that possibility altogether by carrying binoculars.

Do you need to buy a set that

Good binoculars are an indispensible elk hunting tool. Even the keenist eyes can miss distant elk in the shadowed margins between woods and parkland.

will break your bank account? To be sure, some top-line European brands will cost $1,500 or more. If you can afford those prices, go for it, but be aware that you can get a perfectly good set for less than $500. Be aware that you get what you pay for. Anything less than $50 should be used at ball games, operas, and horse races, and certainly not in the hunting woods.

When I'm evaluating binoculars, I look for their functional ability. They absolutely must be waterproof and fog-proof, and I want them to offer clear, crisp focus. I also want good light-gathering capability, and I want them to be as lightweight as possible, otherwise they literally become a pain in the neck. Basically, the higher the power, the greater their light-gathering ability. I

also like the roof-prism model better than the porro-prism. The former has straight, parallel tubes, while the other has offset barrels. I like the roof prism better because of its ergonomic value since it fits my hands well and it balances better when I'm holding it.

It's important to understand how to look. Even the most expensive binoculars won't be of any value if you don't know how to use them. When I glass, I sit in a comfortable place, usually leaning on a tree with my elbows propped on my knees. I'll first look over the area I want to glass with my naked eye, checking for obvious animals. Then I'll determine specific places I want to search. I'll glass those places slowly, looking at the edges of brush, pockets of vegetation, shaded areas, and even obvious places.

I'll look for color as well as parts of an elk. Don't look for the entire form of an animal. When I'm done glassing that spot, I'll turn my attention to another area, and when I'm done, I'll continue with fresh places. Then, if I feel like the area still has potential, I might start all over again, since some animals might have moved to where they can be spotted.

My favorite power is 10, since that's a high magnification and has superb light-gathering capability. At one time, glasses tended to be heavier as the power was increased, but new models these days offer lightweight binoculars that have higher powers. If you want to go really light, small compact glasses will fit nicely in a shirt pocket. Most of them come in six or seven power.

Riflescopes are, in my opinion, absolutely mandatory for elk hunting, even if you're hunting Roosevelt elk in the thick rain forests of the West Coast. Some hunters will disagree, but I've seen too many incidents where there was a need for a scope. In fact, thick cover is one of the places where it's most needed. With a scope, you can thread the needle, so to speak, and pinpoint your target between trees and branches. Open sights might not allow you to do that. Also, as you grow older, your eyes change. You may be a candidate for bifocals, and even if you aren't, it might be difficult to properly line up the front and rear sights.

During hot days, heat waves may hinder a spotting scope's capability...

Scopes come in two styles—fixed power and zoom. Four-power is the most popular and was, in fact, my first scope. It was a Weaver and came mounted on a Winchester Model 70 .30/06 when I purchased the rifle in 1963. Zooms come in a wide range of magnifications, but the most popular is the 3x9. By turning a ring on the scope, you can quickly change to whatever magnification you want. You'll note that the higher the power, the more the crosshairs will dance and waver. That's because the object you're looking at is bigger, and the higher magnification simply makes the wavering seem more intense. The lens closest to your eye is the ocular lens; the one on the other end is the objective lens.

A scope must be fogproof. This requirement is far more important in scopes than binoculars. If the latter fog up, you can still fire your rifle. If your scope fogs, you might as well be carrying a broom, since you won't be able to see through it. Check the warranty offered by the scope manufacturer before you make a purchase. Then test the scope at home by placing it in the bathroom while you shower.

Some scopes can be mounted on a hinge device so they will swing down, allowing you to see the open sights if desired. Other scopes can be mounted so high that you can see the open sights beneath. Be sure that when your scope is mounted it has adequate eye relief. This is the distance from your eye to the ocular lens. If it's too short, you might risk injury when the gun recoils. Many veteran hunters have been "scope-bit." It's happened to me, and it's no fun.

The sighting image in the scope is called the reticule. Simple crosshairs were the earliest reticules and are still popular today, though all sorts of bells and whistles have been added. I like the small dot that sits in the middle of the crosshairs, allowing me to see them easily in low-light situations such as in the early morning or late afternoon. There are also posts—crosshairs that have a varying thickness—and images that allow you to figure a bullet's drop at certain ranges. There are even rangefinders that help you judge the distance to the quarry. Personally, I like a scope that doesn't require you to think, because many elk present themselves when you might have only a few seconds to make a judgment and fire. Waiting too long may cost you a shot.

A spotting scope is valuable when you're hunting elk where there's good visibility, especially if there are point restrictions and you must evaluate antlers from a long distance. Most spotting scopes are heavy and bulky, but there are new models that are lightweight and compact. Spotting scopes have widely variable powers, running up to 60-power or more, and most have zoom capability. Because of the high magnification, scopes must be used on a tripod. Trying to hand hold them is a waste of time.

During hot days, heat waves may hinder a spotting scope's capability, especially if it's turned up to its highest power. Of course, viewing is best done early in the morning and late in the afternoon when elk are most active.

Rangefinders were almost unheard of 10 years ago, but today many hunters use them. They allow you to quickly judge the distance to the quarry, so you won't be making a wild guess and failing to compensate for bullet drop at long yardages.

Binoculars are also vital to spot elk in thick brush or forest cover.

BOWHUNTING

Bowhunting for elk is extremely popular in the West and attracts new hunters each year.

ELK OFFER one of the finest challenges to America's bowhunters. Tree stands are normally not an option, requiring the hunter to be on terra firma with the quarry. Mobility is of paramount importance so the hunter can move as the need arises. Being in good physical condition is an asset, since you might need to quickly negotiate rough terrain at high elevations.

Of course, bowhunting requires the hunter to be close to the quarry, but it's also critical that there be absolutely no obstacle in the path of the arrow. Even the smallest twig might cause a profound deflection if the arrow strikes it. Because you never know where an elk will show up, you can only hope for acceptable shooting lanes that allow you to shoot through. If there are few or none, it's best to quickly find a more acceptable location to call from.

Bowhunters enjoy elk because seasons are always held during the rut, giving the hunter the very important option of vocalizing with the quarry and calling it within bow range, which is about 30 to 35 yards. The ability to call elk in itself is exciting, and one of the biggest thrills in hunting. Hunters also like elk simply because of the animal's charisma and the joy of being in the field in September.

If you're just getting started in bowhunting, buy your equipment from a hands-on archery dealer, where you can be shown several options and be "fitted" for a bow. In those stores the clerks are pros and will answer your questions and measure you for the bow that is best

suited to you. They will also assist you in choosing the appropriate draw length. Many shops also have indoor ranges, where you can try out a variety of bows and receive basic shooting instructions. Other accessories, such as sights, mechanical releases, and other gear can also be evaluated.

As you become familiar with archery equipment, and decide to buy another bow later on, you can then shop for better prices at department stores or make your purchase from a hunting catalog, but nothing beats a pro shop for the initial investment, or, for that matter, a long-term association with that store.

When I first started bowhunting, compound bows were unheard of. My

A bowhunter with a beautiful bull taken in Montana. Despite the snow, this was a mid-September hunt during prime bugling time. All bowhunts occur during the rut.

Jim Zumbo with a bull he took bowhunting in Montana. This bull was shy, but the author's buddy took a position 100 yards behind the author and called the bull within range.

first bow was a Bear semi-recurve, which I purchased in the early 1960s. That particular bow seemed to be by far and away the most popular in those days, and I hunted with it along with firearms as well. I was never exclusively a bowhunter, though I practiced intently with a bow, and enjoyed the challenges of archery hunting.

A few decades ago, compounds came on the scene, and they were initially met with resistance by some hunters who felt like they were too "high-tech," and defeated the very challenges of bowhunting. Proponents argued that compounds offered increased arrow speed, more accuracy, and ease of drawing and shooting, therefore making the compound a more effective and ethical weapon by reducing wounding losses. As the years passed, the compound bow was embraced by the majority of bowhunters, and today it's the bow of choice for most hunters. There are still plenty of hunters, however, who continue to use the semi-recurve as well as the longbow. The latter is a traditional single-limb bow that offers no modern advantages, and, in fact, a fair number of hunters still use wooden or handmade arrows with longbows.

Before modern sights came along, we shot instinctively, which meant we lined up the arrow with the target as we drew the string, and let it fly when it "felt" and "looked" right. This was perfected by hours and hours of practice.

Today, bowsights are commonly used by modern archers. Typically, the quarry is lined up by a peep sight mounted on the string, and pins on the bow, and pinpoint accuracy is virtually assured once you get the knack of it. The pins translate to a different distance and are usually positioned to allow for shots at 10, 20, 30, and 40 yards.

Each year, sighting devices improve dramatically. Some sights have eliminated multiple pins, and you can now mount a rangefinder on your bow to determine the precise distance to the quarry. It's a good idea to upgrade your knowledge by reading new catalogs each year and visiting archery shops to see what's best for you.

The bowhunter is only as good as the performance of his or her arrow. Invest in high-grade arrows that are properly suited to your bow. Modern arrows are made of carbon and aluminum, replacing fiberglass shafts that were popular a couple of decades ago. Prior to that, wooden arrows were used.

The fletching, or feathers on the rear of the arrow, allows the arrow to rotate and stabilizes it in flight. Feathers were

Invest in high-grade arrows that are properly suited to your bow.

once the sole option, but most archers today prefer plastic. While muted colors help the archer and his equipment blend in with the woods, the fletching is an exception. Bright colors allow the arrow to be observed once it flies from the bow, confirming a hit or miss and location of the hit. It's also easier to find a spent arrow on the forest floor if it's fletches are brightly colored.

The broadhead, obviously, is the instrument that ultimately achieves the objective of the bowhunter. It causes the demise of the animal, and must be in perfect working order to quickly and humanely dispatch the quarry. A broadhead may have two or more cutting edges, some of which may be detachable. The most important quality is sharpness. A razor edge is mandatory, and every bowhunter must ensure that this be the case.

When practicing, field tips are used, and they should weigh the same as the broadheads to be used for hunting, since arrows of different weights may fly differently.

Practicing is of paramount importance. No bowhunter should consider going afield unless he or she has the utmost confidence in their shooting ability. The best bowhunters shoot year-round. Many begin practicing in early summer, shooting for at least an hour each day. It's a good idea not to tie yourself into a set period of time to practice, because you may tire and begin shooting poorly. Shoot only as long as your muscles and attitude will allow.

HUNTING GEAR

Make a list to ensure that you haven't forgotten anything before you go on your hunt.

HUNTING EQUIPMENT

Because elk hunting typically requires arduous forays in steep country, and the quarry is large, needing specialized tools to handle and process it in the field, you'll need far more gear than you will when hunting deer.

A fanny pack can hold only a limited amount of gear and is usually too small to accommodate your needs. A daypack, on the other hand, has a greater carrying capacity and will be more useful. Be sure the pack you choose fits well and rides properly on your shoulders. Check that its shoulder straps are wide and well adjusted. The waist strap should fit properly in a snug fashion to keep the pack from bouncing and will also transfer some of the weight of the load to your hips.

Since you'll be carrying it on a hunt, I recommend avoiding any pack constructed of stiff, noisy synthetic material. Your pack should be rated as waterproof, but even so I like to store items such as matches, fire-starting materials, small flashlights, batteries, etc., in zipper-lock plastic bags. Many packs have all sorts of straps and strings attached. Get rid of the ones you don't need; they can be noisy and distracting.

If you're faced with the necessity of backpacking boned meat, several garbage bags will come in handy as a pack liner to keep blood from soiling the pack's contents. If you plan on packing whole quarters, consider a pack frame, convertible pack, or a pack with an oversized pocket to accommodate the quarter.

Rope or some kind of cord is always handy. Rope can be used to hold the elk in position for field dressing and can be needed to tie quarters to a pack frame. If your elk drops on a steep slope, tying a leg or two to a tree will keep it from sliding. If you can transport it, a compact block and tackle will be valuable in lifting meat off the ground so that it can be tied to limbs out of reach of bears and other carnivores.

Meat bags are bulky, but are necessary to contain boned meat or

Make sure you have enough gear to be comfortable in all kinds of weather, and that your equipment is weatherproof.

Make sure everything is in working order before your hunt. You don't want any breakdowns in the woods.

quarters, especially if you have to leave the meat in the field while you get assistance. The bag can be hung from tree branches and the air will circulate through it in the breeze. Cheesecloth can be used in place of meat bags, but it's flimsy, tears easily, and allows flies access through the open weave.

A sharp knife is essential, along with a sharpener. If you plan to bone the elk, take along an extra knife, one with a long, slender, flexible blade. This will allow you to cut meat away from the bones. A saw is necessary if you plan on quartering your elk. Several types of saws are available, the best having a long, flexible blade with a stout handle. Some are small enough to be carried in a belt case. As a rule of thumb, however, more robust saws with a bigger blade are more useful than small ones, enabling you to apply more pressure to make the necessary cuts.

The choice of other gear depends on the weather you expect to encounter, your personal needs, and your hunting strategies. Mandatory items include at least one flashlight (I always carry three small flashlights) and a supply of fresh batteries. You'll also need a good compass, updated topographical map, an extra jacket or shirt for cool weather, and

a small survival kit that includes waterproof matches and match case and first aid items. A canteen or container of water and some kind of trail food are other necessities. Binoculars are invaluable, and a lightweight spotting scope can come in very handy. Optional gear can range from a camera and extra food to bugle and cow calls if you plan to hunt the rut. No doubt you'll want to include other items not listed here. Make an effort to keep your gear as light as possible. Your back will be most appreciative.

PERSONAL
GEAR

As they say in elk country, "If you don't like the weather, give it a minute and it'll change." You can expect snow, hail, rain, wind, heat, and cold (perhaps all in one day), and you must be prepared for it. Of course, when you're packing for your trip, you'll have no idea what to expect, so you're apt to throw in everything but the kitchen sink. If you're headed on a backcountry horseback trip, your outfitter might have weight limitations. If you fly, you'll want to pack accordingly, or pay an airline penalty for excess baggage.

The clothes you choose for your hunt will be determined by the time of year during which you plan to hunt elk. September hunts are generally mild, with clear blue skies and temperatures that average in the 70s or higher. Elk country in September is also subject to thunderstorms, days of drizzle and heavy rains as well as fog and even snow. I've experienced more September blizzards

It's easy to overpack for a hunt. Carefully go through your gear and eliminate items you don't think you'll need, especially if you're riding into camp on horseback.

in the elk woods than I care to remember but fortunately the foul weather generally tends to be short-lived. By late September and early October, however, morning frosts become common. To be on the safe side, bring a selection of both waterproof and warm clothing. As fall progresses, you can expect cold nights, with greater chances of snow. By November, the mountains are in winter readiness, and you must be prepared for sub-zero temperatures and plenty of snow.

When selecting clothing, look for apparel that's made by well-known and reputable makers. Select quality clothing, or you might find yourself wet, cold, and miserable when you're supposed to be enjoying the hunt of a lifetime. Since you'll be hunting in mountain areas where the weather can change quickly, you'll find that layered clothing is the way to go. In the high country you can be enjoying a balmy day, hunting in your shirtsleeves, only to discover that when

the sun dips below the western horizon you'll really need a heavy jacket.

Hunting for elk is a strenuous activity and you will find that perspiration is your worst enemy; avoid it by wearing proper clothing for the occasion. As you hike and climb, you'll start removing excess clothing as you begin to sweat. When you perspire, your undergarments get wet and if the weather cools you'll get chilled very quickly.

For outer garments, I recommend wearing clothes made of wool or synthetic materials that are warm and silent. Wool is probably the very best material to wear during adverse weather—particularly in cold, snowy weather. Goose down is a superb filling for cold weather clothing as long as it's dry and retains its loft. If it gets wet, however, it's a nightmare. It's almost impossible to get it dry in camp unless you can hang it in the sun during a hot spell for several hours. If you prefer down, acquire a Goretex or similar waterproof gar-

BASIC GEAR

HUNTING GEAR
- Binoculars
- Lightweight spotting scope
- Hunting knife
- Bugle and cow calls (if you're hunting during the rut)
- Rope

FIELD DRESSING EQUIPMENT
- Hunting knife
- Boning knife
- Knife sharpener
- Hand saw
- Meat bags

OPTIONAL GEAR
- Camera
- Film
- Extra food
- Zipper type plastic bags

PERSONAL GEAR
- Hunter orange clothing and hat (check local regulations —typically 400 sq. inches)
- Waterproof outer garment (Goretex or similar fabric)
- Jacket (down, wool, or other insulating material)
- Undergarments (long johns polypropylene, chloropropylene, or silk)
- Warm hat
- Gloves
- Boots (select type depending upon expected conditions)
- Socks (polypropylene sock topped with a heavy wool sock)
- Sleeping bag (rated at zero-degrees or lower) if camping

ment to wear over it.

We like to believe that the best materials for outdoor clothing come from nature, but I find that's not necessarily the case. Many modern synthetics outperform natural materials. I have a heavy down jacket that I love to wear during very cold weather, but it becomes useless in the rain.

Cotton, on the other hand, is the worst material to wear in the woods, whether you're wearing it as innerwear, or a shirt, sweater, or jacket. It quickly soaks up water and perspiration, and dries slowly if at all, remaining cold and clammy for long periods of time. Blue jeans are made of cotton and no matter what brand, they're absolutely awful when they get wet and cold. It'll seem to take forever to dry them, and you'll be in pain when they freeze.

The choice of undergarments is important, since they're the closest layer to your skin. Long johns such as those made of synthetics such as polypropylene and chloropropylene and silk are among the best. They come in different colors and are available for both men and women.

As I mentioned, it's extremely important to keep perspiration to a minimum. Of course, this isn't always possible if you're huffing and puffing up a steep slope after an elk, but if you're doing something like splitting firewood in camp, take some clothes off. Once your undergarments get wet with perspiration, you'll have a hard time warming up again if you find yourself having to

It's extremely important to keep perspiration to a minimum.

remain stationary in the cold, such as riding a horse back to camp.

A warm hat is extremely important. Though you might have a special fondness for a certain well-broken-in baseball cap that you got for your birthday, it might cause you to half-freeze to death on your elk hunt. Be aware that in cold weather most of your body heat will escape through a poorly insulated or unprotected head. There's an old saying in the north: "If you want to stay warm, put on a good hat." In extremely cold situations when the wind is blowing hard, wear a balaclava, ski mask, or other facial covering.

Gloves are essential to keep your hands warm. For hiking or sitting still, mittens work well, or even a muff, but you should be able to quickly extricate your shooting hand. When you're choosing gloves, you'll want the type that has an opening or slit for your trigger finger. Applying trigger pressure is an extremely sensitive task; you must be able to feel the trigger since the shot must be perfectly timed with your hold on the target.

Boots are among the most important item of clothing you'll wear. If your feet hurt or get wet and cold, you'll be miserable and unlikely to want to put in a hard day of hunting. Never wear brand-new boots in the field. Break them in well before the season—before they're broken in, boots are usually stiff and can cause sores and blisters if you put them to hard use.

In dry, warm weather lightweight, waterproof boots are fine. I find that you

If you're tent camping, be aware that the fire in your stove will go out soon after you retire. Be sure to bring a warm sleeping bag.

should always think waterproof, even if you expect nothing but fine dry weather. For cold weather, insulated boots are a must. If you expect to hunt in snow, boots having leather uppers and rubber bottoms with felt inserts are a good choice. The felt liners will absorb perspiration as you walk and can be removed in the evening and dried for the next day. I always bring along an extra pair in case the wet ones don't dry by morning. There are a number of boot soles available these days. I like the air-bob type soles because they offer the best traction on slippery ground. The air-bobs are round and about as big as a button. They work amazingly well in snow and on slick slopes when most other types of sole fail.

Socks are extremely important, because they're in direct contact with your feet and boots. In very cold weather, I wear a polypropylene sock topped with a heavy wool sock. In the evening, I dry the socks thoroughly if I intend to wear them the next day. It's best to change to a clean set daily, but that isn't always possible in a backcountry camp where your clothing load must be minimized. It's worth repeating—take care of your feet with proper footwear and boots. You won't be able to function if your feet are in pain.

In very cold country, you can use a variety of body warmers by placing them in a pocket, glove, or sock. Most of these are packaged so that when you open them, sudden contact with the air causes a chemical reaction, and they heat up. These are welcome if you're sitting quietly for a spell or if your hands get cold because you've taken your gloves off. In bitter-

This hunter is comfortable in her bunk, because she packed everything she needed.

ly cold weather, they're welcome any time and most will give off heat for an hour or more, depending on the type.

Before you leave for a hunt always make sure to find out whether hunter orange and how much and what kind is required in the area where you plan to hunt. Some state regulations require that you wear a minimum number of square inches—typically 400—an amount easily covered by a vest. Orange hats or head covering may also be required in addition to the vest or jacket. Wyoming only requires one item of orange clothing; a hat will suffice. In Colorado, on the other hand, you must wear solid orange, and not camo or patterned orange. Even if a state doesn't require orange, it's a good idea to wear it anyway for safety purposes unless you're bowhunting—when orange is never required. Since orange may be your outermost garment for the entire hunt, don't buy a flimsy vest that will rip and make noise. Buy a decent waterproof garment that's quiet and warm.

You'll certainly need a sleeping bag on most hunts. Again, down is wonderful, but miserable when wet. I prefer a synthetic bag rated at zero-degrees or lower. Keep this in mind. The best bags are the most expensive, typically from $200 up. Don't be misled into thinking that just because you have a wood stove in your tent that you'll be comfy all night. Rest assured the fire will go out a couple hours after you're tucked away and the tent interior will quickly approximate the temperature outside.

Bring an empty pillowcase and stuff it with soft clothes. You'll appreciate this luxury item. Bring slippers or moccasins too. They're comfy when you're lounging around camp.

If hunting with an outfitter, ask him for a suggested clothing list. Remember that your warm camp will seem mighty tempting when weather conditions are bad and you're cold and miserable. Not many hunters kill an elk in camp, so do yourself a favor and be as comfortable as you can.

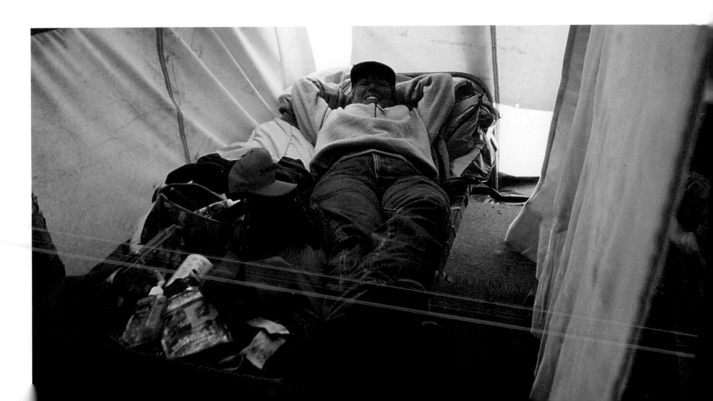

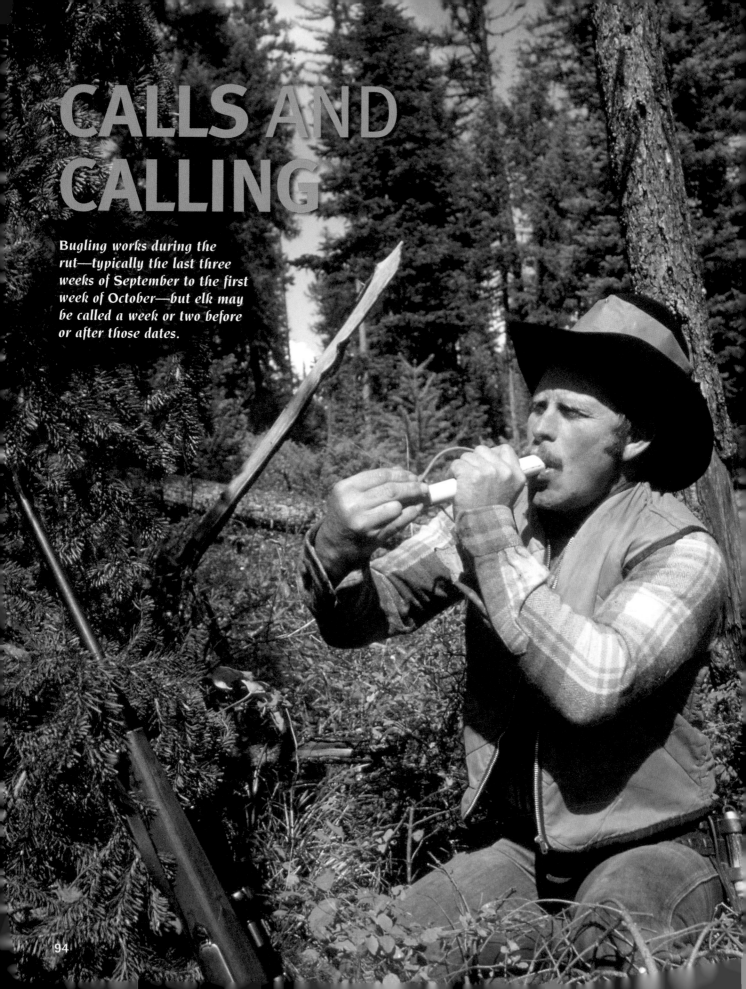

CALLS AND CALLING

Bugling works during the rut—typically the last three weeks of September to the first week of October—but elk may be called a week or two before or after those dates.

BUGLING FOR ELK

Elk calling is often claimed to be an art, a difficult operation that requires much skill. That's bad advice as far as I'm concerned and is one of the greatest myths about elk hunting. Some so-called experts will have you believe that you must create the perfect four-note bugle followed by a series of grunts in order to make a proper presentation to an unsuspecting bull. There's only one problem with that. Most bulls I've known haven't heeded that advice; their bugles range from good to awful if we evaluated them according to our standards.

The bottom line—no two bulls are alike. There is no "perfect" elk call, and no matter how hard we try, we'll never be able to imitate a live bull. As a frequent judge at elk bugling contests, I've heard the champion elk callers. The best of them are very good and come across with "perfect" sounds to human ears, but none can truly imitate the real thing, which is imperfect. In my opinion, the actual call itself is the least important part of trying to entice a bull within shooting range. Far more important is the choice of the calling site, wind direction, and knowledge about elk behavior, especially vocalization, during the bugling season, which occurs from early September to mid-October.

The hunter's call has undergone an amazing evolution over the last 20 years. Store-bought calls emitted a high-pitched shriek that sounded nothing like the real thing. I recall using homemade calls constructed of a short length of garden hose, copper tubing, or a whittled willow branch. Interestingly enough, those calls worked, and still do today.

Then came the diaphragm or "reed" call. In the 1970s, call manufacturer Wayne Carlton discovered that this call, originally intended for turkeys, would make a superb imitation of a bull elk's

A herd bull will go to great lengths to keep his harem together, and may need to fight off other challengers.

bugle. From that day forward, no less than a dozen manufacturers are turning out reed calls. Today, you can find more than six dozen different kinds of elk calls on the market, including a variety that imitate cow elk as well.

Choosing a calling location is the top priority. Obviously, if you aren't in an area within earshot of an elk, nothing happens. Too many hunters select a convenient spot, often a location that's easy to get to and close to a road or trail. We tend to forget that animals live their lives in the territory we temporarily invade and are familiar with human traffic patterns. Smart hunters will put those human places far behind, penetrating hard to reach areas that are away from roads.

If I were looking for a prime calling location, I'd select an area in or around freshly rubbed trees and saplings. Bulls scrape the bark off trees as part of their breeding ritual; these places are often the core of a bull's territory. Disregard rubs alongside trails that are heavily used by people. Elk will avoid spots that are frequented by humans.

Most hunters will make blind calls. This means calling into an area that you assume has a bull elk in it. If you're fortunate, you'll hear a bull sound off early in the morning, allowing you to call with confidence. If animals are silent, which is often the case, a solution is to slip into the hunting area a couple hours before daylight. Being nocturnal, bulls often vocalize in the night, and fall silent toward sunrise. This is especially true in areas where hunting pressure is high. More than once I've pinpointed bulls by listening for them in the dead of night, toting my sleeping bag into a ravine or creek bed where I could listen for nighttime bugling activity.

A big mistake is to assume no bulls are present because

the woods are quiet. Many hunters make a token series of calls and move on to another drainage. I'm a believer in aggressive calling. Before I leave a spot, I'll make a call every 400 to 500 yards, crisscrossing creeks, hiking up to saddles on ridge tops, and penetrating blowdowns. Frequently I've had a bull suddenly sound off after I changed my calling position. I think this happens for several reasons: the bull didn't hear you before, or he responded because you've encroached upon his territory, or he's worked up because you've made him mad with your persistent calling.

When you select a general calling location, pick a spot where an approaching bull won't have to cross an opening. If you're bowhunting, you'll want to set up in an area that has shooting lanes; either natural or those you've cleared. Make your stand in front of cover rather than behind it. It's essential to have freedom of movement to draw your bow when the bull approaches. The same is true if you're using a firearm, though you normally won't need to worry about a close-in shot. Be prepared for any eventuality, since a bull can appear suddenly from any direction. On numerous occasions I've heard a bull several hundred yards off; seconds later he was close enough to hit with a slingshot.

Pay attention to wind direction. Never call downwind, since an approaching elk is likely to pick up your scent. When that happens, it's over. If it appears that the wind is absolutely calm, don't believe it. There's always a slight thermal in the mountains, a wisp of a breeze that will betray you. You can

detect the direction of subtle air motion by lighting a cigarette lighter and observing the flame, or by watching a downy feather attached to your bow or rifle with a thread. I carry a small squeeze bottle of talcum powder that wafts with the wind when sprayed.

Now then, let's assume you've done everything right. You're in your stand, the wind is perfect, and a bull answers your call with a lusty bugle. You call again and the bull responds, but this time he seems to be distancing himself from your location. Another call from your bugle and his response confirms

Beware of the bull that sneaks in silently. He may slip in unseen.

Cow elk make a chirping sound. They're very vocal, and hunters have learned how to use the call effectively for many applications in the elk woods.

your worst suspicions. He's definitely moving away. What to do? The typical reaction from many hunters is to assume they've done something wrong and turned off the bull. More likely, the hunter has performed his or her part correctly, but the bull wasn't interested.

Truth be known, the social status of the bull is the key factor in his willingness to respond. The herd bull with cows may be the most reluctant of all. Consider this: in order to have obtained his harem, he undoubtedly tangled with other bulls, either in a physical antler-shoving match or a bluff. As boss bull, his victory won him the cows that he intends to breed. Along you come, or another bull, issuing a bugle challenge to the herd bull.

A standard reaction is for him to ignore you and escort his girls to safer parts. What he doesn't want is another fight that he might lose. Some herd bulls are aggressive enough that they won't back down

but will temporarily take leave of their cows and sally forth to do battle. This is the mindset you hope for in the herd bull, but is rare.

The solo bull may likewise refuse to rush in to your bugle challenge because more dominant bulls have already intimidated him. All he wants is a cow or two, and not a fight. Solo bulls are often raghorns or two-and-a-half-year-old bulls that are just coming into sexual maturity. They aren't quite fully grown and normally carry modest antlers with four or five points to a side. Conning these reluctant bulls takes some doing. One tactic is to rush the bull, assuming you have plenty of screening cover and the wind is favorable. Bugle as you go, sending the most hateful message that you can. The idea is to invade the bull's territory and get him to come out and fight.

If a bull approaches but won't come in close enough for a shot, leave him alone and come back the next day with a companion. Establish

Judi Zumbo, the author's daughter, with a bull she killed after the author stopped it using a cow call.

a shooter and caller and place the shooter well in front of the caller. When the bull approaches the caller, he may position himself nicely for the shooter who waits silently at the ambush point. Calling elk isn't as difficult as it sounds. If you can breathe, you can blow most modern calls.

THE AMAZING COW CALL

The cow call is without a doubt the most amazing discovery in elk hunting, and I'm proud to say I was indirectly involved in its success, only because I was at the right place at the right time.

It all started in a Montana saloon in 1983, when my friend Don Laubach made a profound remark when he held

up a piece of plastic and made an announcement. "This," he said, "will revolutionize elk hunting."

I had no idea what he was talking about, and I told him to keep talking.

"It's a cow elk call," he said. And then he blew into it, producing a realistic chirp of a cow elk.

Because several of us sitting in the tavern were obviously quite skeptical, Laubach launched into a conversation about why the cow call would work. I'll admit I was far from being convinced, but it was certainly an intriguing concept. Since Laubach's call could simulate a cow or calf elk, this vocalization might have some application in hunting. Maybe. It seemed logical, but the concept was brand new. To our knowledge, no one had ever attempted to imitate a cow elk. It just might work. Laubach gave me a rough prototype, and I was anxious to try it in elk country.

For the next two years I used the call on a dozen elk hunts, and I became a believer, big time. There was no doubt that Laubach's prediction about his call revolutionizing elk hunting was true. Based on my experience with the call, I wrote an article about it in a national hunting publication. Prior to its appearance, I asked Don if he had a few calls ready to go. He and his wife worked part time producing them, and he told me he had about 200 packaged for sale. The article ran in 1986, called: "Elk Hunting's Newest Secret." At the end of the article, readers were told how to order a call through the mail. We all figured that the 200 calls were plenty—imagine our astonishment when the Laubachs received more than 9,000 orders. Not only had Don created a new business, but a new concept in hunting. Elk hunting would never be the same.

Curiously, veteran elk hunters didn't accept the cow call at first. At a Wyoming outfitter's convention, about a year after the story appeared, many old-timers thought the call was just another gadget to rip off hunters. As elk seasons came and went, however, the call percolated into the hands of practically every serious elk hunter, novice and veteran. As expected, other companies began producing cow calls in all sizes and shapes, and by 1990 the cow call was well established.

The cow and calf make a chirping sound and, unknown to plenty of people, so does the bull. This sound is so birdlike that it's easy to be fooled into thinking birds are making the sound. The first time I heard elk chirping, I was a newcomer to the West. It was in the early 60s, and I was hunting mule deer in Utah. I thought I was listening to piñon jays across a canyon when a herd of elk moved into sight. I still made no connection to the elk and the chirps, and finally realized that the animals indeed were making the sound.

What makes the call so amazingly effective? The fact is that elk "talk" all year. Vocalization isn't limited to the rut, which typically occurs in September and early October. During that period, bulls do their bugling, but then it's over. Elk "chirp" the rest of the year, especially when they're feeding or on the move. Bedded elk are seldom vocal.

There's a widespread notion that cows and calves make different chirps, the latter being more high-pitched. Having watched and listened to thousands of elk over the years, not only from my Wyoming mountain home, but in hundreds of hunts around the West, I wouldn't wager that I could honestly identify a cow or calf by its call. Some cows make very shrill, high-pitched calls, and some calves make deeper sounds.

Nowadays some call manufacturers will also claim that vocalizations will vary, depending on the cow's particular mood, such as cows in heat, cows fighting or looking to fight, and on and on. I'm often asked as to the credibility of these claims. I've talked to wildlife experts about elk vocalizations, and I've yet to hear of a study that indicates a cow makes a different sound when she's in heat or participating in a certain activity. Frankly, if a particular call gives you the confidence to use it, then I'm in favor of it. Each year I give elk hunting seminars around the country, and I'm amazed at the number of people who have still not tried a cow call.

I think the primary reason that some elk hunters are reluctant to use the call is because they don't understand it. I'm referring to firearm hunters, since most gun hunts occur long after the rut is over. Bowhunters can pursue elk during the rut; to them the cow call is a must. But it should be a must to gun hunters too.

If you're hunting during the rut, the cow call makes perfectly good sense. Many a herd bull with cows will refuse to respond to a bugle call because he isn't willing to leave his girls for any reason. The bugle call is a challenge to fight, and the herd bull typically runs off with his cows, prodding them away from the intruder. A solo bull may shy away from the

The author took this elk by stopping it with a cow call. Before the author called, the bull was running at top speed with several cows. The call stopped the entire herd in their tracks.

bugle call for the same reason. He's looking for cows and not a skirmish with a rival bull.

Enter the cow call. Many herd bulls can't resist the chirp of an unseen cow, and may run in for a look. Ditto for solo or satellite bulls. A cow is exactly what they're looking for. Hearing it may send them into a frenzy and they're apt to charge straight in.

After the rut is over, bulls begin leaving their harems, and cows may join up in larger herds. Bugling is finished, and this is the time most hunters enter the woods. The opener of the general season signals the beginning of intense hunting pressure. Elk are scattered by hunters, and become largely nocturnal, spending daylight hours in security cover where they're least apt to be disturbed by hunters. Warm weather will also compound the problem; elk will

remain in the cool timber far longer.

You can hunt these "jungled-up" elk, as we call them, by penetrating their lairs. To do so you must make noise. If you're quiet, you surely aren't where the elk are—you're in woods far too open to hide elk, or on a good trail, two-track, or logging road.

So how do you get close to elk if you're noisy? Be aware that elk are also noisy. They can't possibly move silently in dense cover, which means that a certain amount of noise will be tolerated, but it must be natural. You can't get away with wearing clothing that scrapes loudly against brush, and any metallic noises will set off an alarm in the woods.

When elk hear you moving through brush, they'll be at full alert. You can put them at ease by blowing softly on the cow call every 30 seconds or so. When elk hear your cow call, they believe you're another elk walking through the forest. This reassurance will allow you to move closer to their location, which explains why this technique is so effective.

Chances of you spotting the elk first are slim to none. When they realize you're danger, they'll flush in an explosion of hooves, dirt, debris, and flying branches. Here's where the cow call really shines. Blow it as hard as you can, making a shrill sound. Some calls produce a high whistle, others will just make a screeching noise. It doesn't matter. What matters is that 95 percent of the time, every spooked elk will stop in its tracks and look at you. Obviously, it's a whole lot easier to hit a stationary elk than one busting through

the timber. Don't expect the animal to stare very long. You might have no more than five seconds to get off a shot.

Each year, I give elk hunting seminars around the country. I ask my audience how many of them have tried to stop a running elk by blowing hard on a cow call. Invariably, more and more people are claiming they've done it successfully. The reason most hunters haven't is because you must have the confidence that the call will work. But that's not enough. You also must be of the proper mindset to think about the call and use it when all the action is going on. In the excitement of the moment the last thing you might think about is searching for a call in your pocket and blowing it.

To facilitate finding your call during the chaos of elk dashing through the woods, attach a string to it and hang it around your neck. You'll be able to grab it quickly. There's another good reason for the string. If you're using a cylinder-type call, it may freeze up during cold weather. Hang the call under your shirt—your body heat will keep it warm.

It doesn't matter what time of year you try to stop running

This bull was enticed to cross a river, where no hunting was allowed, into a legal hunting zone by Colorado outfitter Westin Clark. A cow call coaxed the bull to cover almost a half mile to the hunter.

elk. The cow call works all the time. The same is true when walking and blowing your call to reassure unseen animals. The key point, to repeat, is that elk vocalize 365 days a year. It can be used successfully regardless of the month you hunt.

Another outstanding use of the call is blowing it to attract animals separated from the main herd, or animals that have been split up. Given the social nature of elk, they group together in bands most of the year. An exception is in the spring when cows go off solo to bear calves. Then they quickly rejoin the herds.

I learned about attracting elk to the cow call on a hunt in eastern Oregon. I was walking through unfamiliar woods when I busted a huge herd, perhaps 80 or 90 animals. They ran off in two different directions (this was before the time I realized that a sharp chirp would stop them), and all fell silent. I sat down to eat an apple, and 10 minutes later I heard a cow chirp. Another cow answered her from a different location. As the calling continued, I wondered if the two herds were trying to rejoin.

The wind was perfect, and I had a hunch. I blew my call softly, and it was answered immediately by a cow, and then another. Soon we had a three-way conversation going. I saw a herd of elk walking toward me, chirping as they came, and I saw another bunch coming from another direction. I had an any-bull tag and was ready to take a spike, but there wasn't a bull in the bunch. But I learned an amazing new strategy, and I instantly became a believer in using the call to entice animals to investigate vocalizations. The ploy has worked many times for me since then.

On another occasion I was hunting in Idaho, and walked up a trail that overlooked a brushy clear-cut. It was mid-morning, and elk would certainly be bedded. I found a vantage point and blew a soft chirp on my cow call, and instantly saw a half-dozen elk get on their feet and look at me. All were cows, and I had a bull tag, but it worked. The curious animals were easy targets had there only been a bull in the bunch.

Calls vary enormously. Some are "bite and blow," where you simply bite down and blow—a simple rubber band reed produces the sound. Other "blow" calls are cylinders that you simply blow into. The standard diaphragm call, shaped like a horseshoe that is seated in the roof of your mouth, is extremely authentic but difficult to master.

There is also a new call that is sort of a small rubber ball that you push with a finger. As it deflates, it produces a chirp. Take your pick, but do use one. Hunting is competitive; and using a cow call will put you on the same page with most other hunters. That may mean the difference in success and failure.

It doesn't matter what time of year you try to stop running elk. The cow call works all the time.

ADVANCED CALLING TECHNIQUES

I've been a judge in many elk bugling contests, including the "Super Bowl contest" which is hosted by the Rocky Mountain Elk Foundation at their annual convention each year. The contestants are very good, some of them outstanding, and many could convince hunters that they're truly live bulls. In fact, many callers can convince live bulls that they're also alive. But some of those callers have no clue as to what to do in the woods when they're calling to bulls and not judges.

Anyone can master an elk call. It's just a simple instrument, one you learn as you would a guitar or piano, but far, far easier. The crucial aspect of calling is in understanding how to interpret the bull's response, and then how to react accordingly. To do that, you must know all about elk—their habits, behavior, and patterns.

I've heard call manufacturers boast that their calls will entice any bull within range. That is absolute nonsense. Those people are simply trying to sell calls, and either have a problem with the truth or know little or nothing about elk. Elk calls have come a long way over the last 25 years. They're far more advanced than early calls, and make a wide array of sounds. But are they really necessary? When I first started calling, I

If a bull hesitates to come in where you can see him and get a shot, try raking a tree with a stick to simulate antlers being scraped on a tree.

used a length of metal hose that was about three feet long and, when coiled several times was about 10 inches long. I also made calls out of garden hose and a wooden stick. They worked in those days and they still work today. What this proves is that an elk will respond to any call that sounds remotely like a bugle. There's one good reason for that: elk also make horrible, off-key calls that sound nothing like what we expect.

One example stands out in my mind. Many years ago, my buddy and I were hunting for mule deer in Utah and we heard a jackass braying in a deep canyon. We were perplexed, because we were a long way from any ranch or livestock and couldn't imagine what a jackass was doing in that remote area. Curious, we made our way into the canyon and eased toward the animal that was still braying. Imagine our surprise when we saw it, but it was a dandy six-point bull elk. Since that incident, I've heard elk make other weird noises, and I'm never surprised when I do.

Does that mean elk are stupid if they respond to a poor call? I don't think so. I believe that since they can't reason, they thereby can't deduce that what they're hearing is bogus since they themselves are constantly listening to all sorts of vocalizations. I do believe, however, that elk can identify different calls by their sound. If you call an elk, for example, and your carelessness causes it to spook, I doubt if you'll ever be able to elicit a response with that

Elk also make horrible, off-key calls that sound nothing like what we expect.

call from that bull again. I also believe that if you call from the same places that other hunters do, elk will recognize the ploy because of the heavy human traffic in that area.

We often hear that elk are call-shy. This usually occurs in places where there's heavy hunting pressure during the rut and elk are so accustomed to hearing people calling that they shut up. When this happens, hunting can be extremely difficult, since the animals are typically impossible to see in the heavy cover they inhabit at that time of year. Without the ability to communicate with elk, there's virtually no way to locate them.

Elk vocalization occurs year-round, which surprises many people. Cows and calves constantly sound off every month of the year with chirping sounds when they're traveling or feeding. But it's in September and early October when the bulls are bugling during the breeding period. That's when we hear elk, which is one of the reasons why we perceive them to be so charismatic and unique to hunt.

Comparatively few firearms hunters have the opportunity of hunting at this time of year, since gun seasons in most states don't open until mid-October or later. On the other hand, bowhunters have the opportunity to hunt elk in every state when the rut is on. Since the requirement of getting close to the quarry is of paramount importance and hunting from tree stands seldom works in heavy forests, the ability to call an elk within bow range is essential. There's an immense difference between bowhunting for elk in a vast mountainous region and hunting a whitetail on a farm where the quarry can be readily patterned.

In some states, the general firearms season opens early enough in October so that hunters can use calls and there are some early muzzleloader seasons as well. Limited entry units in some states may allow September hunting with firearms and there are certain wilderness areas in Idaho, Wyoming, and Montana where there are early September hunts.

Let's say you're fortunate enough to hunt an elk in September. How advanced must your knowledge be to successfully call in a bull? Do you have to be an expert caller and know volumes about elk behavior? To be sure, the more you learn about elk and elk calling will help, but there are some basic steps you should know. Let's look at them, and then examine other options when the elementary techniques don't work.

Don't expect to toot on your elk bugle and then be run over by madly charging bulls. After a lifetime of elk hunting, I can tell you this is the exception rather than the rule. It may happen, but don't count on it. Choose your calling location with two factors in mind. The first is extremely obvious, which is to pick a place where a living, breathing elk can hear you. Then, find a place where you have some visibility, whether you're hunting with a bow or firearm. In the case of the latter, you won't need so many shooting lanes, but you'll still need to see the animal

unobscured by brush.

Don't call from well-used human trails or next to roads. Remember this: elk were born and raised in the forest that you're hunting. They know exactly where people tend to congregate, and will avoid those areas. Instead, penetrate the woods and ease along, calling where you find sign. If you hear a bull, work your way as close as possible before calling.

Elk have territories, and bulls are not happy when another bull enters their backyard. By getting in close, you might fire up a bull that had a case of lockjaw and wouldn't respond when hunters called from a distance or near a road.

I don't know how many times I've been frustrated by hearing nothing but silence on a frosty September morning when you just know bulls should be carrying on, especially in a place that has plenty of elk. I've been deep in wilderness areas during the prime time of the rut when I never heard a peep for days. That's one of the biggest mysteries of elk hunting. Many people have theories, but none matter if you can't get a bull to respond.

I try to make things happen by working my way through the forest, first working the ridges and then dropping down into canyons and timbered draws. I'll bugle every now and then—every 10 minutes or so—and keep working my way along if I get no response. The very best time to do this is early in the morning when the sun is still a long way from the eastern horizon. That's when elk are most active during legal shooting hours.

I remember one hunt when a buddy and I hunted hard, but couldn't

ELK CALLS

PRIMOS
Bugles
"Terminator" Elk Grunt Hose
"Terminator" Elk System
View Larger Photo
Hyper LIP Bugle
LIP Bugle
Cow calls
Hoochie Mama
Hyper LIP Double
Hyper LIP Single
Lead Cow and Calf
Mouth diaphragms
Easy Cow II
Elk Select 4
Hyper Plate
Imperial Plate™
Ivory Plate
Rogue Bull Triple
Royal Elk Double
Sentry Plate

HUNTER SPECIALTIES
Bugles
Challenge Bugle Elk Call
Mega Grunt Tube
Mini Grunt Tube
Li'l Bugle
Mega Li'l Bugle
Cow calls
Estrus Squeeze Me Cow Call
Estrus Whine Reed Calls
Lonesome Cow Call
Mouth diaphrams
Carlton diaphragm calls
Carlton's Classic Premium
Flex Diaphragms
Tone Trough Elk Diaphragm Calls

QUAKER BOY
Bugles
Herd Bull
Challenger Elk Bugle
Cow calls
Herd Master
Hyper Herd Master
Mouth diaphrams
Open Reed Elk Call
Royal Bull
Cow & Calf
Screamin' Green: Loose
Single, Double, Triple, Raspy
Bull

get a response. We dropped into a draw that was choked with a night-mare jungle of downed timber, and I was sure no elk could possibly negotiate its way through that wicked stuff, especially a big bull. We came upon a small spot that had fresh elk droppings, signs of recent feeding on the grass, and several rubbed trees. When we made a call, a bull suddenly exploded from the timber, and charged madly toward us. I killed him with my .30/06, and could have taken him with a bow. That animal wouldn't respond when we bugled from afar, but couldn't stand it when we knocked on his back door.

Hunters often make the big mistake of calling from a high human traffic area such as a well-used road or trail. Get in the woods—the closer you are to the bull's backyard, the more apt he is to come to the call.

One of the biggest problems is trying to entice a herd bull that has a bunch of cows. The majority of bulls in this scenario will ignore you when you make a bugle call, and, in fact, vacate the area, taking their cows with them. This is a no-brainer and should be expected. If you convince the harem master that you're a bull, he'll be most unhappy with the notion that you're a competitor intent on stealing his cows. This goes on every day during the rut. Herd bulls work hard to keep their cows together and well away from other bulls.

So what do you do when a bull takes off over the ridge with his cows, putting as much distance as he can between you? First, realize that unless they're spooked, they might not be traveling very fast. A bull will move only as fast as his cows and will constantly keep them gathered in a group as he moves them along. What you need to do is fool with his brain. His response to your calls, if any, will depend on his mood, aggressiveness, and the status of his cows. In the case of the latter, few bulls will leave a cow that's in estrus in order to challenge another bull, though there are some exceptions.

In Yellowstone National Park, I once watched a big six-point bull guarding his harem of a dozen cows. He was interested in only one cow, which appeared to be in heat. Suddenly, a pair of four-point bulls showed up and pressed in on the big bull. He

Some bulls won't enter an open area in the woods. You might need to set up where there's cover, but be sure you have some shooting lanes or windows.

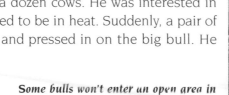

immediately gave pursuit, initially chasing the pair away and then following one for some distance. The second bull took advantage of the big bull's absence and rushed in, successfully breeding with the cow. He left quickly and the big bull dashed back to the cows, unaware of the intruder's deed. I believe the herd bull left his cows because he had visual contact with the smaller bulls, and they were brazen enough to get too close.

If you know the country and the wind is in your favor, try making a big circle to get in front of a bull and his cows if they're headed away. Wait until they're close, and then try a cow call. I've seen many herd bulls that just couldn't resist checking out one more cow, no matter how many ladies they had in their harem. If you can't get in front of the retreating herd, try being aggressive. If the wind is in your face and there's enough

cover, rush the bull, moving as close as you dare without being seen. Many times a bull will draw a line in the stand, so to speak, and hold his ground. He'll refuse to run and come looking for you.

Another technique is to get as close as you can and loudly scrape a branch against the trunk of a tree. At the same time, grab a nearby sapling and shake it vigorously. Make several bugle calls as you do so. You'll be simulating another bull that is frustrated and ready to fight. The bull you're after might get worked up to the point where he'll come looking for you.

Some bulls will hang up and refuse to come close enough where you can get a shot at them. If this happens I'll put away the bugle call and wait 10 minutes or so. Then I'll start cow calling, keeping it up for as long as I believe the bull is around, but at least for about 20 minutes. In

MORE ELK CALLS

KNIGHT & HALE
Bugles
Ex-Tend-a-Tone Elk Bugle
Model 801 Elk Call
Cow calls
Lost Herd Cow/Calf
Model 801 Elk Call
Mouth diaphragms
Double Aspen Elk Diaphragm
Single Spruce Elk Diaphragm
Triple Dark Timber Elk
Diaphragm

LARRY JONES
Bugles
Herd Bull
Challenger Elk Bugle
Cow calls
Herd Master
Hyper Herd Master
Mouth diaphragms
Open Reed Elk Call
Royal Bull
Cow & Calf
Screamin' Green Loose
Single
Screamin' Green Double
Screamin' Green Triple
Screamin' Green Raspy Bull

JONES CALLS
Bugles
Original Jones Elk Call
Jones Persuader Elk Call
Cow calls
Jones Persuader Elk Call
Jones Cow Elk Call
Mouth diaphragms
Small Bull Diaphragm
Medium Bull Diaphragm
Old Bull
Screamer Elk Call

This bull issues a challenge in typical elk country: a beautiful high mountain land that is remote and off-limits to all but the hardiest people.

this case, be on the lookout for the bull to approach silently. He might have been initially intimidated by your bugle, but will ease in close to check out the cow he's hearing. If you're hunting with a partner and the bull hangs up, one of you should approach the reluctant bull as close as possible while the other hunter moves away, cow calling as he goes. The bull will think the cow is leaving, and advance, unaware of the remaining hunter. I've seen bulls run right into the lap of a hunter when this trick is successful.

Cow calling is done not only to lure in bulls, but cows as well—if the cows come, the bulls will follow. I've hunted in the company of many outstanding callers, but Al Morris, a Colorado outfitter known to his friends as "Big Al," is one of the best callers I know. He can quickly interpret what a bunch of elk are doing, and react with a series of cow and bugle calls. He'll chirp nonstop if elk aren't responding, using three or four different cow calls. He believes that different calls send different messages to elk, and his success rate bears out his beliefs.

If a bull has no cows, he's called a satellite or simply a loner bull. This solo animal is mad at the world, since it's breeding season and he's alone. He's not interested in responding to a bugle call, unless he thinks he can

You don't need to be a champion elk caller to be successful.

sneak in and steal a cow. But for the most part, he'll ignore another bull. If he hears a cow, however, he might come unglued and run in to make his claim. That's another instance where a cow call will often work when a bull call won't.

Don't be fooled into thinking that elk will respond to calling only during the rut. You can use a cow call any time by reassuring elk you are merely another animal as you walk through the woods. When you jump an elk, blow on the call sharply. The chances are good that you'll stop the elk in its tracks, providing the opportunity to take a shot. You can use the cow call to attract elk to your location any time of the year.

Recently, I was on a hunting trip with Colorado outfitter Westin Clark. It was October 20, well after the breeding season, but Westin was able to call in a distant bull with his cow call. The bull slowly advanced at least a half-mile, and Westin gradually coaxed him across the shallow river that was the boundary of our hunting unit. I watched as one of Clark's hunters neatly took the bull as he stepped out of the river.

You don't need to be a champion elk caller to be successful. Learn as much as you can about elk. Read books, go to seminars, and attend elk hunting conventions. There's no such thing as too much information.

ELK
SEASONS

During the rut, mature bulls will keep spikes away from cows. A herd bull won't tolerate the presence of any rival bulls near his cows, even spikes.

During the rut, herd bulls, such as this six-point "royal," will concentrate their energy on gathering a harem of cows, breeding, and driving away any possible rivals.

HUNTING THE RUT

Knowledge of elk behavior during the rutting season can be the key to a successful hunt.

It's a pity that most elk hunters never observe elk during the breeding season. That's because most firearms hunts occur in mid- to late October in prime elk states, and the rut is basically over. But it's fascinating to watch elk as they progress from their peaceful summer haunts to early fall, when they're transformed into temperamental, violent animals.

Elk generally congregate in large herds throughout most of the year, with bulls hanging out in bachelor groups that form late in the fall, after the end of the breeding season. As their testosterone levels rise, usually in mid- to late August, they will disassociate with each other and the bulls will lose the velvet that covers their antlers. As the rut intensifies, a bull tries to collect as many cows together as possible to form a harem in order to breed with all of his cows.

At this time, bulls will attack brush and saplings battering them with their antlers, demolishing several saplings each day. Thrashing is not done to rub the velvet off the antlers, as is commonly believed. In fact, the velvet splits in long shreds and is shed quickly, with some assistance from the elk. Most of the velvet will fall away in a day or two, and the bull then continues to vigorously work over the vegetation as a part of his usual breeding behavior. It is thought that bulls display thrashing behavior in order to deposit scent on the saplings from their preorbital glands, either to mark territory or claim dominance over other bulls and cows. Bulls have been observed working over a sapling or brush for several minutes up to a half-hour or more. This practice results in the discoloration of an elk's antlers.

Bulls will frequent wallows during the rutting season. Wallowing is classified as a form of breeding behavior, since it seldom occurs much beyond early October. Bulls roll in the wallow—usually a shallow mud hole—to cake themselves with mud. The bulls urinate in and around the wallow before and during their frolic. They will bugle actively during their wallow and will often thrash nearby brush and saplings.

Wallows can be seeps or springs that are frequented exclusively by elk, or large water holes used as water sources by livestock and other wildlife. Natural wallows can often be found in wet places on mountainsides where water percolates out of the ground, in areas adjacent to creeks in moist valleys and near rivers and beaver ponds. Bulls may visit wallows at any time of the day, but most observers feel that visits are more frequent in the late afternoon and early evening.

The bull's drive to gather a harem of cows intensifies as the rut advances. Bulls bugle to assert dominance and warn off competitors. Two evenly matched bulls will be seen to challenge each other, but stop suddenly and divert their aggression by working over a sapling. Another dominance display is the parallel march, where two bulls trot rapidly next to each other, with one of the bulls eventually running off.

On rare occasions this march can become the precursor to a deadly battle where antlers are used in head-to-head combat. This is not the casual sparring match occasionally exhibited by bulls in the late season, but rather a deadly combat. Typically, the fight ends with one or more broken tines and the retreat of the loser. Death, however, is not common, but can happen when a bull gives in and attempts to retreat. If he falters or is caught in the flank by the triumphant bull, the winner may press his advantage and may kill the downed bull by repeatedly goring it.

A dominant bull isn't necessarily the one with the largest antlers; in fact, he is the one that is the most aggressive. However, since bulls with larger racks are older and more experienced, they are dominant animals and tend to become successful herd bulls.

A cow remains in heat for less than a day, and if she isn't bred, will come back in heat after 21 days. The herd bull will mate with each cow in his harem as she comes into estrus, all the while keeping his cows in a small group well away from challengers. He then shows no more interest in the cow and will be ready to breed with another cow after a brief rest. Cows in a harem will often attempt to escape, perhaps to join another bull or

simply to get away. The herd bull typically dashes after the wayward cows and steers them back to the herd.

In the strenuous process of breeding and tending his cows the harem master sleeps and eats little, remaining constantly on guard to look after his cows. He will lose weight that he must regain before winter sets in. An early, severe winter can be a threat to the survival of many rutting bulls.

Less dominant solo bulls, also known as satellite bulls, will persistently try to sneak in and mate with one of the harem master's cows. This is frequently successful when the herd bull is absent, driving off another satellite bull. A different solo bull, unchallenged by the harem master, runs in and quickly isolates a cow in estrus and mounts her. The mating event itself is very quick with a receptive cow.

Some scientific literature suggests that it is the cow that selects the bull, choosing males with larger antlers. However, I've personally witnessed enough cows bred by small solo bulls during a herd bull's absence that I don't believe that the-

ory. I think that when cows are receptive they will naturally accept any available bull, since time is short during the estrus period.

The breeding period is divided into a pre-, prime, and post-rut. During the pre-rut, bulls interact with cows for the first time, remaining near the harem while trying to attract more to join their herds. Few cows, if any, are in estrus at this time. During the prime rut, cows go in and out of heat daily, and the herd bull tends to them closely, never leaving except to drive off challengers. In the post-rut, most cows have been bred, and bulls may wander away more often to seek other cows.

Cows breed as yearlings and most cows bear a single calf, which is born in the spring. Twinning occurs but is extremely rare. Cows move away from the herd to bear their young, rejoining the group soon afterward. Spike bulls generally stay with their mothers until their second autumn, when they're typically driven off by a herd bull. Spike bulls are sexually mature, but do little breeding. Their testosterone levels are not as strong as those of

In major wintering areas, it's not uncommon for several hundred elk to band together. They'll leave in the spring as the snow recedes in upper elevations.

114

Elk may travel 10 or more miles a day to reach wintering grounds when the snow piles deep in the high country.

older bulls, although on occasion spikes have been known to successfully breed cows if herd bulls are absent. Thus a new cycle begins and the male calves that escape predators become the bulls that we all look for in following years.

LATE SEASON

Elk are champions when it comes to migration, often traveling 100 miles or more to reach wintering grounds from summer ranges. The reason elk migrate at all is purely a matter of survival. As winter comes on, deep snow blankets the high country, effectively sealing off food sources. Elk have no choice—they either descend to lower elevations where there's less snow and available food or perish.

Though I dearly love hunting during the September bugling season, late fall offers the biggest bulls and the easiest access to elk. Herd bulls can be elusive in September, but later they have no choice but to escape the snow and make themselves more accessible, along with all the other elk.

I also love the medium of snow, and one of my fondest strategies is following a smoking hot track in snow. But there's a problem. Not many states offer late hunts that coincide with the migration. Among the top elk states, Montana is a notable exception. Offering a general hunt that extends to late November, when migration is well under way if there's enough snow. And therein lies another problem. During mild winters, elk migrations might be delayed to January or February, or they might not occur at all. That's the risk one takes when hunting migrating animals. Other than Montana, many states offer late hunts that must be drawn in a lottery. Many of those limited entry units offer superb hunting.

Since snow is normally present, elk can be hunted by following tracks. That's not necessarily an easy proposition, even though you're following a big animal that leaves a large impression as it walks. While that's basically true, that's the only easy part of tracking. Elk country is big. Add to that the fact that elk often cover great distances between feeding and bedding areas, and walk for many miles when they're migrating, and you have a major tracking chore.

A toasted sandwich and a cheery campfire provide some comfort during lunchtime on a cold day.

There are three fundamental ways to locate elk tracks. Of course, you can watch the elk making them in the distance, and then start tracking after you work your way over to locate the prints. Using a spotting scope or good binoculars you can easily see tracks in the snow in openings where elk have fed or traveled at night (bright sunshine helps since tracks are more difficult to spot in shade). Finally, you can find tracks as you walk through the woods.

Whatever your track locating method, you should prepare for a long hike. Elk that are casually moving back and forth between feeding and bedding areas provide the shortest tracking session, though they may move over considerable distances when hunter pressure is heavy. The longest tracking effort will be the pursuit of migrating animals that may walk 10 miles or more in a day or night. In between are the elk that are pushed by hunters and are headed for another spot within their home range.

You can generally identify a fresh track because the edges will be crisp in soft snow. If the tracks are frozen, they're probably hours or even days old. In powder the snow falls back into the track and doesn't allow any comparisons; it is difficult, if not impossible, to tell the age of a track. One method is to press your foot into the snow near a track and lift it out to compare the appearance.

Other clues might help you tell, such as urine or droppings that haven't frozen yet, or droppings on top of snow, indicating that they're as old as the last snowfall. Check whether the droppings are frozen; warm droppings will thaw snow under them, sinking a bit. If the dropping is warm to the touch and the air temperature is very cold, unsling your rifle and get ready for a shot—your elk is very close ahead.

Tracking, of course, demands quiet clothing. Avoid noisy synthetic waterproof jackets. Wool is my

Because elk are in lower elevations due to snow levels in the high country, they're often more accessible to hunters.

favorite fabric when hunting in snow. It's silent and keeps you warm even when wet. Animals are acutely aware of sounds behind them. If the snow is icy making silent tracking impossible, make a wide circle to intercept the animals as long as the tracks are fresh. Partially thawed and refrozen snow will be so noisy that you'd be wise to abandon tracking. Try a technique where you din't need to move, such as watching from an ambush point near a trail or feeding area.

You'll need to try and figure out what the elk that you are following are up to. Meandering and seemingly aimless tracks can indicate that the elk are getting ready to bed down. As you move, be alert for any unexpected color or shape. If you spot an elk, stop moving immediately and take stock of the situation. Carefully use your binoculars to identify the animal. Even if it's an elk that doesn't interest you, use your glasses to scan every foot of the forest for others. Move cautiously and keep glassing as long as the elk are not alerted to your presence. If the animals flush, you can use a cow call to stop them.

Tracking can offer a sense of false security. We know that the elk are up ahead and become overconfident. We move along too fast, or fail to properly search ahead. Many tracking efforts end up with elk breaking out of cover, or in failing to catch up to the elk at all. You'll be following big animals in big country, and you'll soon learn that they aren't pushovers.

Proper clothing is essential to keep warm when the temperature is at zero or lower. Wool is one of the favorite materials for snow and cold.

This hunter took his bull during the general Colorado rifle season, which is a time of very heavy hunting pressure. He did it by letting crowds push elk to him.

THE **TOUGHEST** SEASON

Newcomers to elk country are often shocked when they arrive at their hunting spot on public land and find it crawling with hunters. There's an old joke that you need sunglasses to hunt elk in such places—not because of the bright sunlight, but to ward off the reflection of all the hunter orange.

Crowds are at their worst during the general firearms season, particularly in those states that offer unlimited tags. Hunters concentrate in popular spots where elk numbers and harvests are high. Of course, elk harvests are high there because so many people hunt the area. In fact, the percentage of hunters taking elk is probably lower than in areas where there are fewer elk and less hunters, since the quality of bulls is often better in low-pressure areas. Heavy pressure keeps elk moving and removes more legal bulls from the herd, leaving fewer available animals.

It's obvious that competition is the name of the game when we hunt. That's true regardless of the species we pursue. Think about it. If you were fishing, for example, you could catch fish even though anglers were lined up shoulder to shoulder, as long as the fish were running. But if you're hunting, the last sight you want to see is someone else's pickup parked at your spot. They say that the early bird gets the worm, but that's not necessarily true when hunting in a crowded spot. Quite often it's the smartest bird that gets the worm.

One way to avoid crowds is to go the extra mile. Get up a couple hours earlier and walk a little farther. You'll be surprised how few hunters are reluctant to get very far away from a road or trail.

During general seasons, elk hide in heavy cover and change their daily behavior patterns. They'll often bed in the most rugged, heavily timbered country they can find.

This hunter heads as far away from a road as he can to beat the crowds. It's always best to put some distance from the crowds if you don't like being around other hunters.

If you can tolerate crowds, a good strategy is to let them work for you. Set up at the edge of thick cover where elk seek refuge. Trails will show where elk travel, and if you find intersections, set up close by and stay there all day. That's essential, because hunters typically move around in midmorning when they're hungry, bored, or cold.

Another way to beat crowds is to hunt on the fringes of traditional elk country. In many areas, the lower elevations support piñon-juniper forests. These forests can be hundreds of thousands of acres, or just a few hundred. Elk commonly inhabit the forest, but many hunters pass them by, eager to reach the upper elevations where the elk are expected to be.

Heavy hunting pressure alters elk behavior dramatically. If you locate elk herds prior to the season, don't count on them being there on opening day. As the season nears, hunters move in, setting up camps, cutting firewood, roaring around in pickups, and otherwise alert-

ing elk. The animals know long before the opening day that the woods close to roads are not safe. They'll seek cover and change their patterns overnight. Instead of feeding openly in meadows, they become nocturnal, feeding and moving in darkness. They'll hide by day in the thickest cover they can find. Often bedding in thick blowdowns and thickets near the top of very steep ridges.

Scrub oak is another type of cover that is generally shunned by hunters, primarily because it's nasty to get around in, and it's often assumed that elk don't live there since it doesn't look like elk country. The best way to hunt the oak brush is to climb high on an opposing slope and look down into it. Elk often feed in grassy areas near the brush and retreat into it at daybreak.

Remember that hunting pressure alters elk behavior to the point where you may rarely see an animal during legal shooting hours. If you really want an elk, you'll need to hunt longer, harder, and smarter—especially the latter.

The author took this bull in a crowded woods by sitting between escape cover and feeding areas. Other hunters pushed this elk right into his lap.

HUNTING
THE **BACK** COUNTRY

No form of wheeled transportation is allowed in wilderness areas. You are allowed to travel only by foot or on horseback.

Once you enter a wilderness area, forget about all the conveniences of civilization. You'll never experience a more primitive way of living.

HUNTING THE WILDERNESS

In 1964, the United States Congress passed a wonderful piece of legislation that created the American wilderness system. Enormous chunks of remote country were designated as wilderness areas in national forests. These areas were established to preserve the last of our primitive lands, where no logging, mining, or other civilized exploits could be done. No roads could be built, and no internal combustion engines could be used, ruling out chain saws and generators. No pesky, noisy inventions that create electrical power and detract from the primeval ambiance that existed before we became a high-tech society.

In a wilderness, you can stand on a ridge top and look off in the distance. Stands of timber roll away as far as you can see—uncut forests that will never be felled by man's hand. No roads will scar the valleys and bottoms; no dams will plug the streams and no utility lines will ever mar the landscape. You will never see a track made by a wheel—any kind of wheel, whether it be part of a mountain bike, cart, or one of man's confounded machines.

The wilderness has been described countless times by writers who try to relate the unique "feel" of such places to their readers. Their descriptions can't convey what you really feel. You must experience it firsthand to enjoy the incredible mountain splendor, to rejoice in the tranquillity of an outdoor cathe-

Portable lanterns are the only permissible light sources for use in wilderness areas since no gasoline-powered generators are allowed.

Jim Zumbo with a bull he took in a Colorado wilderness area.

122

dral that has never been exploited. While we can walk in any woods and feel an inner peace, whether it's in Central Park or some other metropolitan setting, nothing quite matches the sensation of a true wilderness.

Hunting in the western wilderness is severely limited for obvious reasons. Access can consist of a wretched journey through tortuous and twisted trails, and is almost always accomplished on horseback. Very few big game hunters try wilderness hunting on foot because of the need to transport a very heavy cargo of elk meat back to civilization. Whereas fishermen, hikers, and photographers commonly tramp about the wilderness, their needs are simple and cannot compare to those of the big game hunter.

My first real backcountry hunt was in Montana's Anaconda Pintler Wilderness. I was so excited I could hardly believe it was actually happening. I drove to a small nearby town, met the outfitter, other hunters and guides, and we kicked off the voyage with a bit of celebration in the local saloon. The local folks were a friendly bunch, many of them kidding me about the big wild and woolly trip I was about to go on.

We were in pickups the next morning long before daybreak, loaded with gear and towing horse trailers. We arrived at the trailhead a couple hours later and the sun was peeking over the eastern mountains when we climbed into the saddles. I'd been on many horses before, and had done a great deal of riding in the mountains, but never into a bona fide wilderness area.

An hour later I saw a small wooden sign next to the trail, indicating the boundary of the wilderness. The sign was small and crudely printed, but its message was huge and powerful. Beyond this point, I'd be in a sanctuary, a place where progress isn't measured by the number of shopping malls or housing developments, but rather by how many miles you travel in a day, or how much firewood

you manage to cut.

Every view was spectacular, whether it was along part of the trail that wound out of the timber and along a steep slope, or in the very bowels of the forest, where alders grew thickly, over-towered by huge Engelmann spruce that had been growing there for hundreds of years.

I smelled the smoke long before I saw camp. We rounded a bend and I saw my home for the next seven days—four wall tents pitched in a lovely glade surrounded by lodgepole pines. The cook was already in camp, having ridden in the day before, and was concocting a wonderful stew.

We were shown around the cook tent, which would also serve as our dining room, and in just a short time our gear was unloaded from the packhorses. The sleeping tents were equipped with cots, a wood stove, and a small pile of cut firewood. A lantern hung from a wire connected to the ridgepole, and a ground cloth provided a dry floor.

With our sleeping bags spread on the cots and our gear stowed, I walked around to explore the surroundings. I kept thinking about the exquisite area, and couldn't quite get over the permanence of the landscape. Here, finally, was a place that man could not destroy.

The cook showed me the spring that supplied our water, and the natural pasture where our hobbled horses grazed contentedly. The grass was thick and lush, and the horses fed voraciously, making up for calories lost on the arduous trek into camp.

Suddenly the outfitter shouted, and I turned to see him staring up at one of the rocky pinnacles that

loomed high above us. He pointed out a white object perched precariously on a ledge. A mountain goat was basking in the sun. Someone produced a spotting scope, and we took turns looking at the white animal in his unbelievably rugged environment.

Lunch was served, and we enjoyed a fine bowl of stew. Though food always tastes better when you're camping, this stew would have been a hit in a five-star restaurant. We had the rest of the afternoon to loaf around, since elk season didn't start until morning. It was unseasonably hot, even at our high elevation, and weather was the main subject of talk around camp. Our outfitter was concerned, indicating that our work would be cut out for us. The elk would be elusive as ever, seldom very far from the cool recesses of the thickest forest.

As it turned out, the hunt was unsuccessful in terms of bringing home an elk. The weather was too nice, with blue skies, starry nights, but much too warm for elk hunting. But I was so impressed with the week in the wilderness that it mattered not at all that I didn't get a

Horses are indispensable when hunting in a wilderness area. Unless you have your own, you'll need to rent or borrow horses. Simply walking into a wilderness area is tough enough, but if you get an elk you'll face a logistical nightmare.

Horses are almost worth their weight in gold when it comes to packing out several hundred pounds of elk meat.

shot at an elk. If the hunt could be gauged by satisfaction and enjoyment, then it was a raging success.

When you hunt in a wilderness, consider that any hunt in the backcountry will require a major physical effort. Horses may not be able to go where the elk are because of the nature of the terrain, or because of the disturbance factor. Astute hunters tie their steeds as soon as is practical, and slip about afoot, often climbing very steep, timber-clogged slopes.

Thousands of outfitters operate in elk country, many of them specializing in wilderness hunts. If you are tough enough to try an elk hunt in a wilderness area without horses, you had better think two or three times about your capability of not only moving your camp in and out of the mountains, but transporting out several hundred pounds of

meat if you're successful. This isn't an impossible task. I've done it myself, but it's likely to be the toughest hunt you've ever been on in your life.

As an added bonus (as if a wilderness elk hunt requires extra motivation or cajoling), many backcountry areas offer an early rifle season starting in early or mid-September. To an elk hunter, that spells rut, or breeding season, the time that bulls create a symphony of music across the great beyond. There, in the opinion of this author, and many others, lies the quintessence of hunting. Nothing, absolutely nothing, compares to an elk hunt in the lands that will remain forever wild. Finally, a wilderness experience seems to forge a common bond with those who participate. Don't be surprised if you make long-term relationships with the outfitter, guides, and other hunters in camp.

HUNTING ON HORSEBACK

Horses allow hunters to reach remote destinations and leave the crowds far behind.

Horses can be a tremendous asset on an elk hunt for two important reasons: they'll get you to where the elk are with a minimum of physical discomfort, and they'll also carry your elk out of the woods. The latter is a profound luxury.

I've owned a number of horses and have ridden countless others. I've had a couple mishaps, but only because I took some avoidable risks. A horse is a surefooted animal and wants to live as much as you do. In rough country, a horse will make his way where he feels comfortable, though you might foolishly lead it into a dangerous place where the ground is unstable, steep and icy, or too hazardous.

I recall many hunts where we put our horses into places that seemed impossible. One such hunt was in Canada where we crossed a bog single file, with me in the rear. The horses had to step precisely onto hummocks that offered some solid ground. Everyone made it through nicely except me. My horse missed a hummock and landed in muck that seemed to have no bottom. I flew out of the stirrups, no worse for wear, except for my red face. To add insult to injury, my horse did exactly the same thing on the way back.

When you hunt on horseback, you will either use your own horse, a pal's, you'll rent them, or you'll be with an outfitter. If you use your own, you'll obviously be in good shape since you're familiar with the animal. Using a buddy's is no reason to worry because your pal should know the horse's habits and tell you what you need to know. A rental horse can be a big problem because you don't know its history and peculiarities. Be sure to ask about the horse when you rent it. If you're with an outfitter, he should have a trusted horse to carry you safely around the mountains.

Riding is simple. Before you head out, check your stirrup length. Do this by standing in them. If you feel comfortable, you should be okay. If they seem too short or too long, adjust them accordingly. You'll be riding a western saddle, which has a horn in front. That horn is used to tie your halter rope to, and offers something extra to hang on to if you wish.

The halter rope is used to lead the horse or to tie it up. Never tie up with the reins. Tying a horse to a tree or even

a corral post is a bit tricky. You need to know the correct knot, and the length of rope the horse needs to be comfortable. Leave this up to your guide or an experienced hunter.

Directing the horse is done simply with the reins. To turn left, merely raise both reins and pull slightly from the left with slight pressure, and the same with the right. Resist the tendency to turn left by pulling on the left rein. It doesn't work that way. You must use both. To assure that your reins won't slip and fall to the ground, tie a knot in them. If you drop them, they'll stay in place on the horse's neck.

You'll probably have saddlebags; stow items in them that you might want to get at quickly, such as water, gloves, extra film, etc. The rear of the saddle will have a pair of leather straps to tie on a waterproof coat.

Hiring packhorses makes it easier to carry sufficient gear into the roadless backcountry.

Packing is an art and a science. It takes skill and experience to properly rig a packload onto a horse.

Never carry your gun slung over your shoulder while you're riding. It will beat you up as you move along, and you'll constantly need to adjust it. Use a scabbard, which attaches to the straps. Some outfitters put them on the right side, but that's unwieldy since practically everyone dismounts from the left. In the event you need to get out of the saddle to take a quick shot, you have to leap off, run around the front, and jerk your rifle out of the scabbard. Make it easier and attach the scabbard on the left side.

Never, ever, shoot while you're in the saddle. You might see this in the movies, but that's about the only place it's done. Those Hollywood horses are trained to allow a shot to be taken above heads. Years ago, when I was guiding mule deer hunters in Utah, a hunter asked me if he could shoot from his horse. I told him that was a profound no-no, but he did it anyway a couple days later. A nifty little rodeo instantly occurred and the man ended up sitting on the ground with a sore butt.

Many mountain horses are trained to allow you to dismount on either side. This enables you to lift yourself into the saddle from the uphill side without turning the horse around, and is especially handy on narrow trails. Always mount from the uphill side. If your horse is positioned so you can't do it, turn the animal around if you're like me and have a decided preference to mount from the left side. Even a slight slope is deceiving. You may find that trying to mount from the downhill side will require you to raise your leg another foot or more to get in the saddle.

If you feel your saddle slipping to one side while you're riding, try this trick. Jerk your body in the opposite direction, nudging your saddle to the center. If that doesn't work, dismount and tighten your saddle or ask your guide to do it. Some clever horses will take a deep breath when

One of the greatest advantages of having a horse is to haul meat to camp.

the saddle is strapped on and tightened. Once the saddle is attached, they'll exhale and loosen the strap.

If you're in for a long ride, make it easier on yourself and walk your horse downhill from time to time. You'll be able to exercise sore muscles and give the horse a break as well. When riding down a steep slope, sit high and lean back in the saddle, adjusting your weight to help the horse. When riding uphill, lean as far forward as possible. On a really steep slope you can grab the horse's mane.

Never use hard suit-cases on a horseback trip, always use a duffle bag. They're soft and can be packed much easier. Keep your gear within the limits suggested by the outfitter. Pay special attention to your sleeping bag and make sure it's in a water-proof bag of some sort. Even though all the gear will be covered with a tarp, moisture can seep in, and an accident on the trail can result in bags rolling and bouncing about.

Smaller items will be packed in panniers, which are boxes or sturdy canvas bags that hang from the packsaddle. The panniers must be balanced, so each weighs almost the same; if not, a rock placed in the light pannier will help even things out. If you carry a backpack, you can either carry it over your back or hang it from the saddle horn.

Horses have all kinds of personalities. If the animal is unfamiliar to you, inquire as to its quirks. Some horses are jumpers. Instead of walking over a log or small creek, they'll make a mighty leap. You should know this in advance. Other horses are easily spooked, jumping a bit

Horses have all kinds of personalities.

if they walk near a light-colored stump, strange rock, or other scary object. Some horses move only at one speed—very slow motion. It will continually lag behind the others, and then trot to catch up, and repeat the process all day. Correct this habit by carrying a small switch. Lightly tap the horse's flank and you'll get an instant reaction.

You'll be riding the horse in the dark when you go on your daily hunts, typically leaving camp long before the first hint of gray in the east and returning long after dark. Don't be concerned when you can't see your hand in front of your face. Your horse has excellent night vision and will carry you safely. Protect your eyes from unseen branches by wearing safety glasses.

Don't fret about your horseback trip. I've never seen a serious injury after riding horses for almost 40 years across all sorts of terrain. My most serious mishap occurred when I rode down a steep icy trail in the dark. The horse went down, and I leaped out of the saddle and sprained my ankle. It was my fault; I shouldn't have ridden down that trail. Make sure your boots slip easily in and out of the stirrups. You don't want them to get stuck if you need to vacate the saddle in an emergency.

If you see a part of the trail that looks frightening to you and the horses ahead are having some difficulty, get off and walk. No one will call you a sissy if you're being prudent. Once you've ridden a while, you'll become much more comfortable. Enjoy the ride; no doubt you'll have plenty of pleasant memories.

HOW TO AVOID GETTING LOST

Always check your surroundings when you move about with no sun to guide you, so you can figure out how to get back to a road or your vehicle.

This bull lived all his life in the woods and he knows the forest well. We are temporary visitors; it's tough for us to find our way around where there are few landmarks and heavy timber.

STUDIES SHOW that 75 percent of foot hunters never venture more than a mile from a road. There are three good reasons for that. Penetrating the timbered mountain terrain is not for the weak of mind or body. I mean really penetrating, where you leave the roads and trails far behind.

One reason can be chalked up to physical conditioning. Many people simply aren't in shape to do it, or they're lazy. It's one thing to walk along a trail, but quite another to actually strike off into the forest and negotiate your way up steep slopes and heavy timber and over ridges and down nasty drainages. For this reason, elk hunting is considered to be, day in and day out, the toughest big game effort in North America.

Another reason makes perfectly good sense. Why would anyone get far enough away from a road when, if they shoot an elk, they would be faced with the profound ordeal of transporting several hundred pounds of meat an inch farther than they have to?

Finally, plenty of folks don't wander very far from roads

It is easy to become disoriented in heavy timber such as this expanse of fir and spruce. If you get lost, the first rule is to keep calm, panic can quickly combine with exhaustion and exposure to produce a deadly crisis.

because they fear getting lost. Elk country is so vast that you can easily get turned around in the timber. The answer, of course, is to hunt places where getting lost is virtually impossible, or, better yet, know how to use a map and compass. A Global Positioning System (GPS) unit will help you unravel the woods, but it has an inherent problem – it runs on a battery. If you've managed to reach Lost Meadow by using your GPS unit and it conks out, you may be spending a lot of time at Lost Meadow watching for a rescue party unless you can find your way out on your own. Always take a back-up compass and map.

Here are some ways to hunt where you're virtually assured of getting out without a compass. Choose a slope where a road runs a long way below it. Obviously, you can hunt the slope all day and simply descend to find the road. Be careful, however, if you top out over the ridge and keep going, walking over other ridges. Then the friendly road might not be so easy to find any more. You can do the same with a creek. Hunt above it all day, and drop down to it when it's time to go to camp. If you really need a visual, follow a fence line. Many forests and ranches have fences to keep livestock controlled. A power line also can be a guide, and might in fact attract elk, since these wide openings often have plenty of feed not found in the timber. If you are still uneasy when you leave your vehicle, try hunting in an area close enough to a busy highway where you can hear traffic all day. I know one urban hunter who does that all the time, and he's actually killed a couple elk. On calm days, you can hear traffic a mile or more away.

But the good old compass is still the way to go if you're serious and want deep penetration in the woods. Learning to use a compass is simple, and it's a comfort to know that the needle always points north, unless a close-by metal object attracts the magnetized needle. Get a book that explains how to use a compass (a Boy Scout handbook is excellent) and practice in your yard, then go to a nearby wooded area and use it. You'll be amazed how easy it is. With a compass and a map, you can find any spot you want.

Elk country is so vast that you can easily get turned around in the timber.

A simple way to use it is to pick a fairly straight road, determine the direction the road runs, and take a bearing toward the way you want to hunt. When you return, you take the opposite bearing back. For example, say the road is running north and south. You strike off to the east, and at day's end you head west. This is a basic example, but it works. You don't need to fret while you're hunting about being turned around and getting out of the woods in the dark.

Many years ago, when I was a teenager attending forestry college in northern New York State, two pals and I took a boat far up a remote lake and went deer hunting. We had no compass and were just a bit overconfident in our ability to negotiate the woods. After all, we were foresters—and teenagers—and thought we were infallible.

We hunted in a dismal black spruce swamp, with isolated hardwood ridges,

These western Washington hunters check their compasses to determine their route in the thick forest.

and there was a local tale that some hunters went in there, got lost, and were never seen alive again. About 10 in the morning we decided to find another spot because there was little sign where we hunted. When we started to walk to the boat, we each walked in a different direction. After a short discussion, we decided to try each person's route.

Soon we were totally baffled and hopelessly lost. One of my companions was on the edge of hysteria and started crying. His distress actually strengthened my other buddy and me and we tried again to find the boat, but we had no clue where to start. Suddenly we heard rifle shots nearby and headed for them immediately. Luckily, we came upon two local hunters who had shot at a bear that we'd spooked toward them. They told us where the lake was, and my pals and I walked out in 20 minutes.

Since that terrifying day, I've never again gone into strange woods without a compass. Sometimes even

a familiar place needs a compass, too. My father-in-law, who had an uncanny sense of direction, was once completely turned around in a 20-acre field that was adjacent to his house during an extremely thick fog.

A GPS unit works like a charm. About the size of a cellular telephone, the unit gets a fix by triangulating between three satellites. Many years ago, at my elk hunting seminars, I asked my audience how many of them had GPS units. Typically only two or three hands went up because early on the units were extremely expensive, usually in the four digit figures. Nowadays when I ask, half the audience has one. A good unit can now be purchased at less then $100. As I mentioned before, and I'll say it again, any battery-powered device can fail. Always take a compass too, if you believe in Murphy's Law like I do.

While it might seem that reading a map is easy, it's surprising how many people don't know that the top of the map is always north. Look for

MANDATORY SURVIVAL GEAR

DAYPACK WITH
- Compass
- Updated map
- Waterproof matches or fire starter
- Waterproof match container
- Fire-starting materials (tinder)
- Flashlight with extra fresh batteries
- First-aid kit
- Container of water
- Trail food
- Extra jacket or shirt
- Plastic trash bag as waterproof pack liner

the legend on the map. It will tell you what the various symbols mean. The scale will tell you how much distance an inch covers, and contour lines describe the terrain. Contour lines that are very close together and almost touching signify a cliff or extremely steep slope. Widely spaced contours show more rolling, gentle terrain.

Some maps show land ownership; typically, national forests are green, state lands are blue, BLM lands are yellow, and private lands are white. Be aware that in some states, it's incumbent on the hunter to know where property lines are. Some states don't require landowners to post their property; others do. A good, updated map is essential, but you must know how to use it as well Don't rely on fences to indicate property lines. Some may be confusing, since they may be only drift fences to keep livestock regulated.

By knowing where you are at all times you'll avoid being cited for trespass if you're in an area where public and private lands mingle. And when you're in the deep timber, knowing where you are will allow you to concentrate on hunting instead of continually wondering where you are and where the truck is parked. Elk hunting is difficult enough.

Let's assume the unthinkable—you somehow get lost. You're alone, night is coming on, and the evening chill creeps in as the sun disappears over the western horizon. What to do? The textbooks say to remain calm and assess the situation. I think those textbook authors have never been lost. It's good advice,

Don't rely on fences to indicate property lines.

and quite correct, but the human brain has no calming tendency when you're in a near state of panic or hysteria.

I think it's important, when you decide you're hopelessly lost, to think about a very basic fact: someone will soon be looking for you. The lone exception is if you're hunting solo for several days, but few people do that. Knowing that you'll be the center of much attention very quickly should be a calming factor. The best thing to do is to stay where you are and quickly get a fire going. With that done, gather enough firewood to last the night for two reasons: you'll likely need the heat, and a fire is wonderfully reassuring.

When daylight arrives, place green branches on the fire to create plenty of smoke and stay where you are. You might try to climb a tree or high ridge to look for clues as to your location, but always be sure you can get back to the fire. That's your only anchor to the world at that point in time.

If help still doesn't come and you know something about the drainages in the area, a last-ditch effort is to walk downstream along a creek or river. Eventually, you'll come to a bridge, road, or house, even if you're in a wilderness area. At some point that waterway must lead you out. There are a few rare exceptions—the creek you're following might suddenly disappear underground, or it might lead into a large swamp.

Getting lost is a terrifying ordeal, as I related above. Do everything you can to prevent it. That's one memory that you won't want to have.

TROPHY BULL OR EASY ELK?

This is the famous Plute elk taken in Colorado around 1900. For more than 90 years it was the world record elk. Owner Ed Rozman poses with the bull close to where John Plute shot it.

THE TROPHY BULL

Not many hunters will ever see a trophy elk. That's a sad commentary, but very true. But let's define a trophy so we can all be on the same page. To some hunters, any elk is a trophy, since a trophy is in the mind of the beholder. A modest size bull taken during a grueling hunt can be more of a trophy that a mega bull shot within 10 feet of a pickup truck. Even a cow elk can be a trophy to some folks. In the most popular sense of the word, however, a trophy is a big bull, a mature animal with impressive antlers. In some areas, a bull that scores 300 B&C is a tremendous trophy. Any bull that scores 340 B&C or better, in my eyes, is a giant and the ultimate is the bull that scores 375 B&C, making the minimum entry for the record book.

Few animals possess the charisma and beauty of a truly big bull elk. The long, sweeping antlers studded with six or more tines on each will impress the most hardened hunter. A trophy is an elusive quarry if he's hunted on wild lands where other hunters pursue him and he has plenty of room to roam. That's the typical scenario on public lands, especially in wilderness areas. Many large mountainous units seemingly have plenty of wild country but support no really big bulls. That's because hunting pressure is heavy, access is too good, and elk don't live much beyond three years. If you want a trophy, avoid those places and look elsewhere. If you must have a guaranteed trophy, you'll need to deal with a game farm

The author took this big bull late in the general Montana season outside Yellowstone National Park. Early snowfall forced the elk down into hunting areas.

This big bull was taken on public land just outside the Yellowstone National Park near Gardiner, Montana.

BOONE & CROCKETT WORLD RECORD ELK

TYPICAL AMERICAN ELK
Score: 442 5/8   *Date:* 1968
Location: White Mts., Arizona
Hunter: Alonzo Winters
Key Measurements:
- Length of main beam:
  Right 56 2/8 - Left 56 2/8
- Inside spread: 47 4/8
- Circ. of smallest place
  between 1st & 2nd points:
  Right 11 - Left 10 2/8
- Number of points:
  Right 6 - Left 7

NONTYPICAL AMERICAN ELK
Score: 465 2/8   *Date:* 1994
Location: Upper Arrow Lake, BC
Hunter: Picked Up
Key Measurements:
- Length of main beam:
  Right 49 2/8 - Left 46 3/8
- Inside spread: 51 1/8
- Circ. of smallest place
  between 1st & 2nd points:
  Right 8 5/8 - Left 8 6/8
- Number of points:
  Right 9 - Left 11

ROOSEVELT ELK
Score: 404 6/8   *Date:* 2002
Location: Benton County, OR
Hunter/Owner: Jason S. Ballard
Key Measurements:
- Length of main beam:
  Right 54 1/8 - Left 57 5/8
- Inside spread: 40 6/8
- Circ. of smallest place
  between 1st & 2nd points:
  Right 8 2/8 - Left 9 4/8
- Number of points:
  Right 9 - Left 8

TULE ELK
Score: 351   *Date:* 1990
Location: Solano County, CA
Hunter: Quentin Hughes
Key Measurements:
- Length of main beam:
  Right 48 6/8 - Left 47 4/8
- Inside spread: 51 3/8
- Circ. of smallest place
  between 1st & 2nd points:
  Right 7 1/8 - Left 6 4/8
- Number of points:
  Right 9 - Left 9

operator who will show you plenty of animals to shoot. These are not wild elk, and they cannot qualify for the Boone & Crockett record book, since that organization views enclosures as unfair chase hunts.

Big bulls are also found on large, unfenced ranches and Indian reservations. Significant numbers are located in Arizona, New Mexico, southern Colorado, and Utah. These are typically expensive forays, with some of the better places requiring a five-digit hunting fee. Some of the top reservations support enormous bulls—the average antler scores run right at 350, which is phenomenal.

Other options are limited entry units where hunting pressure is restricted, thus allowing more animals to survive and live longer. All you need to do is draw a tag, and you can hunt many of these units on public land without an outfitter. Bonus and preference points in many states help you improve the odds of drawing a tag.

Wilderness areas have enough vast country to hide and shelter elk, allowing bulls enough age to grow trophy antlers. Of course, access in a wilderness is almost always by horse. If you don't have horses, you may opt to hire an outfitter.

Some of the most economical trophy units are adjacent to national parks where elk wander out onto public land, usually when snow forces them out. Yellowstone National Park is a prime place. There are excellent late season hunts in both Wyoming and Montana, which allow hunters to take a crack at big bulls. Odds on drawing the tags are tough, but if you get one you may take the bull of your dreams.

Age is the critical factor in the production of oversize antlers. While good nutrition and genes play a role, neither of those two essentials come into play unless a bull lives at least to age five or older. A bull will be in his prime at age seven or older. Since so few bulls live beyond age three on public lands with good access, six-point bulls are rare. In many states, less than five percent of the bulls taken wear six-point antlers. Many large areas have no big bulls and a five-pointer may be king of the mountain. Be prepared to squeeze the trigger when a four-pointer walks by.

A truly big bull will have main beams that are at least four feet long, with the royals, or fourth points, being a minimum of 18 inches. The third points, normally the weakest, will be at least a foot long, and the eyeguards and second points will have a length of about 14 inches. The sur-royal, which is the fifth and last tine off the main six-point beam, will be 10 inches or better.

A handful of hunters achieve the lofty goal of taking a B&C bull, since fewer than two dozen bulls will make the record book each hunting season. But most hunters, like me, subscribe to the adage: "Any bull elk is a good bull elk."

HOW TO GET AN EASY ELK

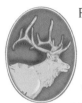

For years I've given seminars on how to get an easy elk. Many hunters acquainted with elk and elk hunting who hadn't yet attended my seminar roll their eyes and grin, suggesting that I'm a little touched. But it's true. There is such a thing as an easy elk. Make no mistake—of all the animals I've hunted in North America, elk get my vote as the toughest.

Goats live in more treacherous terrain, whitetails are smarter, moose are bigger, but day in and day out, an elk hunt on public land without the services of an outfitter can be downright miserable. Even with an outfitter's assistance, plenty of hunters go home each year without an elk. To be specific, if you average all the western states, 25 percent of the total elk hunters are successful. That might not seem too bad, but look at it from another perspective: 75 out of 100 hunters don't get an elk each year.

Making a kill isn't a requirement of having a successful hunt. Plenty of folks who hunt elk country end their hunt smiling, whether they get an elk or not. Just to be in the high elevations with the associated sights, sounds, and smells is enough of a reward.

But the fact is, the objective of a hunt is indeed to bag an elk. If you've got a bull tag, you obviously would love a crack at the Boss Bull of the Woods.

Unfortunately, few of us get that chance, because elk are too often living in impossible country and staying under cover during shooting hours. Most of us who hunt elk with more than casual interest have been outsmarted and frustrated more than we care to admit. Elk hunting often becomes an ordeal, an endurance contest that pushes our bodies to the limit. Every year we may swear off elk hunting forever, but we know we don't really mean it.

With this being the case, is there really such a thing as an easy elk? Many folks will argue that the critter doesn't exist. They claim that no elk is easy. I suppose that depends on how you define "easy." It's a relative term, depending on what you compare it with. My intent here is to look at the elk hunt from every angle, delving into it intensely and determining all the ways it can be done. I'm convinced that the easy hunt exists, but again, it's all a matter of perspective.

A major consideration in defining the easy hunt is the necessity of transporting the elk from where it fell to a road or vehicle. No matter how much or how little effort you've expended, you must deal with a carcass that can weigh up to a half-ton. Removing several hundred pounds of meat is not usually easy, especially if your quarry lies in the bottom of a roadless canyon and your vehicle

The quality of a trophy is in the eye of the beholder. This bull will never make the record book, but look at the smiles on the faces of the hunter and his buddies.

is parked on top of the ridge.

So to truly define an easy hunt, we must first deal with getting the meat out. We're putting the cart before the horse, because we aren't yet considering the effort to get a shot at the elk in the first place. In terms of physical effort, meat removal is almost always the cause of most misery. Of course, the easiest way to do this is to hire someone else to do it for you. Enter the outfitter, guide, wrangler, or packer. You pay him for his services; your elk ends up magically at the meat processing plant or at your front door.

One way to gain an easy elk is to hire outfitters to take care of most of your needs, and hopefully get you into good elk country. The word "hopefully" implies that there's a bit of a question here and indeed there is. Elk hunting can be so unpredictable that you may hire one of the top outfitters in the country and still go home with no elk. All sorts of factors, primarily weather, can work against you. Your "easy" outfitted hunt, whether you're successful or not, may end up being a major ordeal, particularly if you're on a backcountry wilderness trip.

To some folks, the requirement of sitting atop a horse for several hours is a huge effort. Then you must consider the need to follow a guide on foot through steep mountains every day. Chances are your guide will be a tough cowboy much younger than you, who asks that you perform the impossible by just staying within sight of him. You may find yourself sitting on a big rock, gasping for air in the oxygen-depleted high country, rubbing fatigued muscles, and wondering what in the world you're doing there. You'll quickly learn that mountain elk hunting is far from easy.

Another option is to sign on with an outfitter who hunts private land where

you can get around nicely in a four-wheel drive vehicle and shoot your elk fairly close to a road. Many outstanding hunts are available on Indian reservations, most of them in Arizona and New Mexico, or on large ranches that are located in every western state. Be aware, though, that some private ranch hunts may not be everything they're cracked up to be. For example, New Mexico has five 5-day hunts each fall. If you book into the fourth hunt, and have no snow to move elk around, you may see few, if any, decent bulls, most of them having been shot or thoroughly spooked by earlier hunters. It happens all the time.

The bottom line in buying your hunt is to have reasonable expectations. Be willing to come home with something less than you anticipated, though that's tough when you're spending good money on a hunt. With the exception of game farm hunts, no outfitter should guarantee a hunt. If he does, you should take a hard look at his operation.

Another way to get an easy elk is to simply be lucky. The best case scenario is to walk out of your tent or camper, spot an elk sneaking along, and shoot it next to your pickup truck. That, unfortunately, doesn't happen very often, but most of us have heard of cases where lucky incidents occur.

I was told about a hunt that began with a lengthy poker game the evening before opening day. The participants got little sleep that night, and all but one doggedly got up at the prescribed time and headed for the woods before daybreak. The holdout remained in his sleeping bag until midmorning; crawled into his truck around noon, and drove a half mile down the road, where he pulled over and fell asleep in the cab.

An hour later, he woke up to see a

grand six-point bull trotting toward him, whereupon the hunter eased out of his truck, rested his rifle on a fence post, and downed the elk. With help from other passing hunters, he loaded the bull in his truck, winched it up a tree branch next to camp, and had dinner ready when his pals got in that night. Imagine their surprise when they returned to that scene, especially since none of them had seen so much as a spike bull that day.

On a Colorado hunt with General Chuck Yeager, we had to cope with blizzards and poor visibility. Elk hunting was practically shut down, but one morning, while I walked away from camp, a small herd of elk ran down a ridge toward me. One of them was a five-point bull that I immediately collected, counting myself extremely lucky to see any elk. Unbeknown to me at the time, Chuck had kicked the elk off the ridge, and I happened to be at the right place at the right time. The bull cooperated nicely by falling 20 yards away from the road.

Another way to get an easy elk is to "win" it. By applying for one of the many limited entry elk tags offered in all states, you can beat the dismal general season odds and have an opportunity at a good bull. Happily, many of these units are in accessible areas. Landowners residing in those units are quite often willing to allow free access, or they might charge a modest fee. Since the tags are issued

Another way to get an easy elk is to "win" it.

in a computer draw they can't lease their lands to groups as they commonly do in general hunt areas.

You'd think that hunters would be chomping at the bit to apply for these limited entry tags, but it's surprising how few take advantage of the opportunity. For the last 15 years I've been giving seminars on western big game hunting. At the Kingdome Show in Seattle, I routinely show a slide of 22 mature bulls in a single herd. The audience typically gasps at sight of these bulls, and commonly believes that the elk were photographed in Yellowstone or another prime elk area. They're shocked when I tell them the bulls were photographed near Mount Saint Helens, which is just a two-hour drive from downtown Seattle. They're also amazed that the bulls were photographed in a hunting unit during hunting season.

The bulls inhabit a limited entry unit with a very high hunter success rate, far higher than the general hunt rate. Yet less than five percent of the hunters in the audience claim that they apply for those outstanding limited areas.

I think there are a few reasons why this is so. Many hunters believe they're too unlucky to draw a tag. They don't bother filling out the application. Some hunters don't want to hunt an unfamiliar area, preferring instead to hunt the same units with their pals that they've

been hunting for years. Other hunters are so fed up with some of the complicated application forms that they simply refuse to consider limited entry hunts.

To help draw a tag, many states now offer preference or bonus points. The concepts are simple. The preference point system awards a point if you fail to draw a tag. The points accumulate each year until you have enough to draw a tag. No longer is luck a matter of winning a tag; it's simply perseverance. On the downside, some of the units are popular enough that it might take several years to draw a tag.

Some years ago, I drew a limited entry elk tag in Colorado after having accumulated four points. The hunt was in relatively low country, had plenty of access and much of the unit was public land,

where I camped. I took a nice six-point bull after having passed up several others. The elk fell within 200 yards of a road, and I saw only a couple other hunters that day. Other than the cost of the nonresident tag and some food and gasoline, I had no major expenditures.

This might not seem to be terribly exciting, but it is when you consider that elk hunting on Colorado's public lands is woefully crowded with hordes of hunters. As chances of seeing a mature six-point bull are slim to none in heavily hunted areas, you'd appreciate the ease with which I took my bull. Interestingly enough, I make the same survey among my audiences in Denver as I do in Seattle, and very few hunters apply for those units. This baffles me, especially since Colorado offers the win-

win preference point system.

Some states give bonus points if you don't draw a tag. These points also accumulate, but instead of being applied to one application as the preference points are, each bonus point allows an extra application in the hopper. In other words, if you have three bonus points, you have three applications working for you in the computer. Obviously, your odds greatly increase as your bonus points accumulate. This system allows anyone to draw, even the first year. First-year draws are usually impossible with high demand units going to hunters with available preference points.

A basic premise in elk hunting is the very clear fact that competition among hunters is a primary reason that success rates are low. And if you're looking for a mature bull, you might have a long search on public land in general units. It's quite possible that there are no mature bulls where you hunt, because they simply don't live long enough. It takes several years for an elk to develop massive antlers; in many heavily hunted areas, a three-year-old bull is ancient.

Another aspect of getting an easy elk, or even in getting any elk, is knowing about elk behavior. It's always a good idea to know the habits of your quarry, as well as the place he calls home. Your success rate will improve markedly once you understand and become familiar with behavioral characteristics of elk.

There are three basic periods in which we hunt elk, according to state laws and available seasons. They are the rut, transition, and migration periods. Don't be deluded into thinking that just because you're going on a September elk hunt during the prime rut period that you'll be up to your neck in bugling bulls. You might very well hear or see no elk, depending on local populations, hunter competition, and the weather. Remember, too, that the biggest herd bulls might be reluctant to come in to your bugle call, preferring instead to sneak off with their cows.

The transition period, which is the time between the rut and serious snowstorms, is the toughest time to go, and will be the most difficult time of all. This is when elk are done breeding and are in heavy timber, hiding from hunters. This is also the time that most states open their general seasons to rifle hunters.

My choice of periods for big bulls is late, when migrations are under way. This can also be an easy hunt, but many variables are involved. Elk may travel more than 50 miles to winter ranges, making them more accessible in lowland areas. Of course, heavy snow can't be counted on, which is required for a successful late hunt if you're counting on animals being in lower elevations.

As I already mentioned, the toughest part of any elk hunt will likely be the need to transport heavy loads of meat. If you're doing this yourself, you can make it a bit easier by hiring a packer to bring it out, or renting a horse and doing it yourself. Be sure you're knowledgeable around horses and that your horses are indeed trained to carry meat. Another option is to wheel the meat out on a one-wheel carrier. It's a great deal easier to

Take care of your trophy antlers. The author works on a nice bull taken in an Idaho wilderness area. Because these areas don't have much hunting pressure, bulls live older and grow trophy antlers.

144

wheel something rather than to drag or carry it. The toughest option is packing the meat out on your back, either a quarter at a time or boned.

The physical aspect of elk hunting is a deterrent to many hunters, but some take their chances and are sorry later. The best-case scenario is to have a few aching muscles. The worst-case scenario is to be shuttled to an emergency room because you foolishly over exerted yourself in rugged country where the air is much thinner.

Assume that every elk hunt is not easy, even if you've booked an outfitter, and act accordingly. And when you're planning that dream hunt and you intend to do it on your own, seriously consider the limited entry offerings. If you draw, you might very well have an easy hunt. In the elk woods, they come few and far between. And if you have an easy hunt, remember it well, because all the rest might be downright tough.

GAME FARM ELK

This book is all about elk hunting, and I literally mean hunting! I'm ruling out elk confined by high fences, because that's not hunting—it's simply shooting. Ask most elk hunters why they like to pursue elk, and you'll get a variety of answers. The love of being in elk country will be a primary reason and other responses range from the physical and mental challenge of the hunt to the nature of the animal itself. An elk carries an air of charismatic nobility; it is a handsome animal that bears magnificent antlers and its flesh is incredibly delicious.

For those who must own an elk and have no interest in all the associated aspects of the wild hunt, it is possible to buy an animal and shoot it in an enclosure. Again, as I mentioned above, I said shoot and not hunt—there is a world of difference. Elk are raised in pens for several reasons. Some are slaughtered and their meat sold to restaurants while others are raised for their antlers. Some elk are also bred to develop superior genes, while others are raised simply to be shot.

Typically, owners of penned elk never use the word "pen" when they advertise. They refer to their operations as "game ranches," "elk ranches," or "preserves." In fact these penned animals are held in an area surrounded by a high fence, typically seven feet high or more. Invariably, their ads will say their hunts are 100 percent guaranteed, no license is required, and there is no season. Of course, hunters will only be interested when bulls' antlers are hard and shed of velvet, normally from September to March or so. The ads may also proclaim the B&C scores of the elk you can expect to shoot, proudly announcing the trophies that are waiting for you. The shoots are not cheap, ranging from $5,000 and up.

What the ads don't tell you is that their elk cannot qualify for the Boone & Crockett Club because the enclosure violates one of the B&C rules for fair chase. The B&C record book states: "To make use of the following methods shall be deemed unfair chase and unsportsman-like, and any trophy obtained by use of such means is disqualified from entry. ...Hunting game confined by artificial barriers, including escape-proof fencing; or hunting game transplanted solely for the purpose of commercial shooting."

If the prestigious Boone & Crockett Club holds that hunting in an enclosure violates fair chase rules, can that be interpreted to mean that it's unfair to hunt in an enclosure? What we have here is an ethical consideration. Every human has his or her set of values. To some, elk are simply one quarry among many. The notion of hunting an elk in its wild surroundings is not important, and may not even occur to those who hunt in pens.

It's difficult for enthusiastic elk hunters to understand the mentality of those who are satisfied with shooting a penned elk. A tame elk in an enclosure is so far removed from his wild brethren that there's no comparison.

In all fairness, it's understandable why some people might choose to resort to game farms. I refer to those who are physically disabled or have a severe medical condition. That being said there are hunts available in most states where wild elk can be pursued with a minimum of discomfort. I recall an outfitter who, with a pair of guides, carried a hunter profoundly disabled with MS to a ground blind overlooking a water hole. The man was comfortably situated in his wheelchair; left on his own without a guide, and in a couple hours downed a fine bull. This was a bona fide wild elk hunt, with no confining fences.

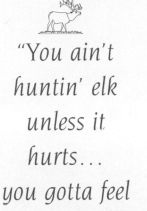

"You ain't huntin' elk unless it hurts... you gotta feel pain."

What does the nonhunting public think about all this? In two words: not much. It's a documented fact that nonhunters are more prone to accept hunting if the participants use woods skills and work hard to find the quarry. A big turn off to the nonhunter is the person who takes shortcuts, relies excessively on modern technology, and hunts in an unsportsman-like manner.

Perhaps the best way to summarize this issue is to quote a veteran elk hunter I met 30 years ago. "You ain't huntin' elk unless it hurts," he said "you gotta feel pain." To that, let me add a comment. You "gotta" see the beauty of elk country and experience all of it. You need to use your brain to outsmart your animal, and when you get blood on your hands, and beat yourself half to death moving several hundred pounds of meat out of the woods, then you'll know what elk hunting is all about. That's something that the people in the pen will never understand.

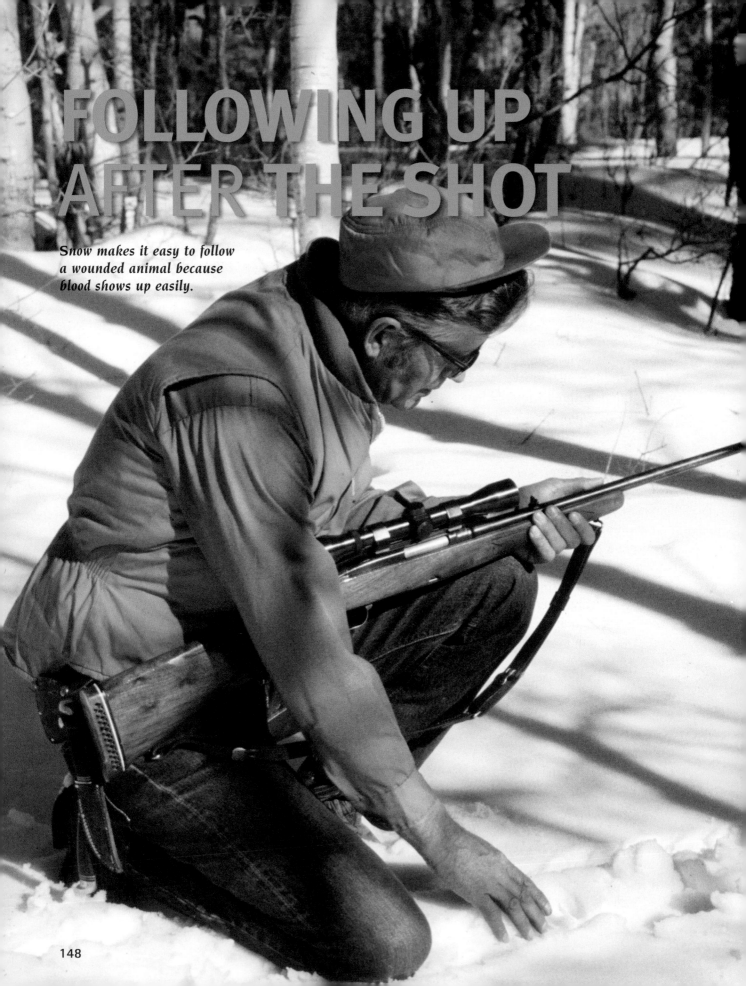

FOLLOWING UP
AFTER THE SHOT

Snow makes it easy to follow a wounded animal because blood shows up easily.

148

A HUNTER'S worst nightmare is hitting an animal and not immediately recovering it. Unfortunately, if you hunt very much, that will no doubt eventually happen to you.

Elk are tough and tenacious and are well known for running out of the zip code if hit improperly. Unfortunately, too many hunters don't recognize a hit or a miss, and if they wound an animal, have no idea how to pursue it. Beware of the animal that goes down instantly at the shot. This usually means three things—it has been struck in the spine, which immobilizes it instantly, or possibly through both shoulders, which will typically put it down on the spot, or it's temporarily stunned and may run off and get away.

I've had instances where animals were struck, went down at the spot, and ran off, requiring a very long pursuit to catch up. That being the case, I'm always ready for a follow-up shot when the quarry hits the ground. I'll stay where I originally shot from, trying to maintain eye contact with the fallen animal, and keeping my rifle ready for a shot if it gets up.

The shot I like best is directly behind the shoulder, in the crease that's usually easy to see. The bullet will take out both lungs. If I have the opportunity, I'll wait until the animal takes a step or two so the off shoulder isn't in line with the bullet. If it's in line, your bullet will damage it severely and you'll lose plenty of meat that didn't have to be destroyed.

Elk are so tenacious they may just stand rooted to the spot when struck in the vitals. Sometimes you'll detect a shudder or slight lurch when they're hit, and sometimes you'll observe absolutely

so sign of a hit. Even if you think you made a double-lung shot, and can in fact SEE the wound, shoot again.

I once hit a big bull perfectly behind the shoulder with my .30/06. He never flinched, and I saw, through my scope, a small red spot precisely where I'd aimed. The bull was dead on his feet, but he didn't know it. I fired again and hit him in the same spot. This time he staggered a bit, but still showed no sign of going down. I put one more shot in the same place, and he fell in a heap. I could have covered up those three entry holes with a tennis ball.

One of the biggest mistakes I've observed is the unforgivable sin of not going to the spot where the quarry stood and making a serious and intense effort at locating a sign of a hit. I mean really looking, and not simply taking a cursory glance if no obvious blood is present.

Besides blood, some hair might be present that was cut by the bullet. You'll probably need to get down on your hands and knees to spot hair, as well as tiny drops of blood that you might not see if you're standing up. Don't just look at the ground; be sure to carefully inspect the tops and sides of grass stems, saplings, and foliage. Many times a betraying sprinkle or smear of blood will be on vegetation rather than the forest floor.

As I mentioned, the quarry's reaction at the shot might provide clues. Some almost guarantee a hit. If an animal kicks out with its hind legs, you can generally wager that it was hit in the heart. Don't be surprised if it runs 100 yards or more before expiring. If an animal humps up at the shot, it's likely a gut shot. You'll have a long haul to locate it again if no snow is

The author took this bull at a distance, but couldn't find it after a two-hour search. There was no sign of a hit. He persisted and returned an hour later and found the bull lying dead 84 yards from where it was shot, concealed in a clump of spruce trees.

present, since there might be little bleeding. Always be suspicious if the animal staggers, lurches, stumbles, or shudders at the shot. It's probably hit, but be aware that sometimes the quarry might jump if a bullet hits the ground beneath it or it's sprayed with dirt or rock chips. Whatever the case, always look. Most importantly, always remember that blood doesn't have to be present to signify a hit.

I'll never forget an elk hunt in British Columbia where I fired at a distant bull and saw him lurch slightly at the shot. The bull ran into heavy timber, and I thought I heard it crash to the ground, but I couldn't be sure. There was no blood or hair where the bull stood, but we searched for two hours, combing the forest, fanning out and making circles up to 300 yards away. But it was no use. The bull was gone, swallowed up in the forest. My guide convinced me I'd missed, and I reluctantly left.

What happened next was an unforgettable event. We were climb-ing away from the spot, headed toward camp, when I had a bizarre sense of recall. The image of the bull formed in my mind, and I could clearly see him lurch and hear the thump in the forest. I blurted out to my guide that the bull was dead, and I was going to find it. The man thought I was loco, but told me he'd wait while I looked one more time.

I charged back down the mountain, guided by some unexplainable urging. Don't ask me how or why, but I ran directly to the dead bull. He had fallen in a clump of spruces, landing on his belly in a depression. The spruce branches had closed back in after he had come to rest, and the only thing I could see were the very tips of his antlers sticking out of the foliage.

Out of curiosity, I backtracked to where I'd shot, and found no trace of blood. The bullet took him squarely behind the shoulder and the elk had run 84 yards before collapsing.

If blood is present, certain clues may help you in determining where the bullet hit. Frothy blood typically means a lung shot. Bright blood may indicate a muscle wound or heart shot. Bits of undigested food are bad news; your quarry has been struck in the stomach or intestines and you'll have a difficult search. If you find fragments of bone, the animal may have been hit in one of its legs.

There are divided opinions concerning the merits of quickly following up on a wounded animal or waiting an hour or so. I think it depends on the clues that you find and the severity of the wound. By allowing an animal to move away without giving immediate pursuit, you allow it the opportunity to bed down fairly close to where it was hit.

Your next move would be to slip along and administer a finishing shot without the animal seeing you first. That can be a major undertaking because a wounded animal will have an eagle eye on its back trail. It's possible that the animal might not be hit hard enough at the initial shot to bed down. In the latter case, it may make more sense to follow as fast as you can to catch up and make a killing shot.

I once shot at a big whitetail buck, only to have a branch deflect my bullet. The deer was hit in the knee, but the leg wasn't broken. Snow allowed me to follow, and though blood wasn't copious, it was regular, provided I kept the deer moving and allowed the wound to bleed. I trotted after the deer, and several hours

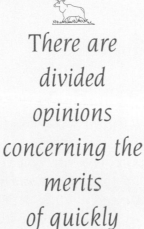

There are divided opinions concerning the merits of quickly following up on a wounded animal...

later caught up with him and put him down. He had simply run out of blood.

It's imperative to locate the precise spot where the quarry stood when you shot at it. This isn't easy to do, especially if you lose sight of the spot when making your approach. Before you move, try to fix the spot in your head using obvious features such as a yellow sapling, large bush, rock, or any distinctive landmark.

Following the trail may call for a very disciplined search where you're totally focused looking for the tiniest amount of blood. Always mark the trail as you go, either with squares of toilet tissue, or plastic flagging (that you should remove later). If you lose the trail, keep trying. Look back at the route you've marked, and try to imagine where the animal might have gone. If it jumped a log or bush or blowdown, look intently, because blood is often lost from the jolt of leaping. Look off the ground on the sides of trees, tips of brush, and grass heads.

If you're on a slope and visibility is fairly open, you can have a companion dog the trail while you parallel him from a higher elevation where you'll have a better vantage point for another shot. Don't give up until you've exhausted every possibility. We should do everything we possibly can to avoid that misfortune. Search and search, and search some more. Give it everything you've got, and you'll sleep better that night.

FIELD TO FREEZER

Dragging an elk is almost out of the question unless you have several helpers and the route is all downhill.

GETTING **YOUR** ELK **OUT** OF THE **WOODS**

 One of my most pro-found memories was staring down at my first really big elk, and wondering why in the world I squeezed the trigger. I was overwhelmed with its size, and knew I was in for a major ordeal. Almost a quarter-ton of meat had to be packed to my truck, which was parked a mile away, and on top of a ridge.

Once the feeling of helplessness passes, you suddenly feel mighty proud of yourself. You gaze upon the forest floor and cannot believe a motionless elk is lying there. The enormity of what has just happened tugs at you, and ever so slowly, reality settles in. In the next few hours you must become a meat processor and head into a journey that ultimately will end at your freezer. Consider your challenge. Before you lays a huge animal three or four times bigger than any deer you've ever taken. You must immediately dress it, allowing the meat to cool as quickly as possible, and somehow get that immense amount of freight out of the woods.

You tag your prize, take a few pictures, and begin the enormous ordeal. Finally you manage to remove the entrails, amazed at their bulk and weight. Next you proceed to skin the carcass, and then begin to dismantle the elk into pieces that you can manage. All the while you keep the meat as clean as possible, and place each portion in the shade to cool more rapidly. Depending on the method you've used, you might have sawed the carcass into four quarters, or perhaps you cut the quarters off at the joints with a knife. Maybe you completely boned the animal, eliminating the need to haul out unwanted bones, fat, and gristle.

The next task is the one that separates elk hunters from deer hunters. Whereas in the case of the latter you can often grab an antler and drag, the elk requires far more planning, gear, and muscles to move it, even a few yards. I can recall many, many times when I was not a happy camper because I dropped an elk where I did. These are always instances when the truck is parked on top of a ridge and the elk lies in the bottom of a canyon three miles away. There's an old saying that suggests that some elk should be eaten where they fell, requiring that a frying pan and a bit of salt, pepper, and cook-

It takes two horses to carry one big elk.
Be sure the loads are balanced and secure.

GETTING YOUR
ELK OUT OF **THE WOODS**

FIELD DRESSING AND QUARTERING
- Hunting or skinning knife
- Boning knife with a long, slender, flexible blade
- Hand saw with a long, flexible blade and stout handle
- Butchering and boning cheat-sheet
- Meat bags
- Knife sharpener

MOVING
Man packing:
- Sturdy packframe or carrier with padded straps and waist belt (average bull elk quarter weighs between 80- and 100 pounds)
- Rope, strapping or parachute cord
- One-wheel carrier or cart (not permitted in wilderness areas)
- Lightweight portable pulley system to shift and hang game (conditions permitting)

Horse packing:
- Horses (two horses for one elk)
- Packsaddles, tack and harness
- Rope

This woman takes pride in field dressing her own elk.

ing oil be included in every backpack.

When you come right down to it, you're looking at a grand piano laying on the ground, or at least the equivalent. Your job is to manipulate a carcass that can weigh 800 pounds or more. It must be nudged, pushed, and shoved so you can remove the innards, not an easy task if the animal is lying on its belly and you're either alone or with a pal who has a bad back.

I remember one particular instance where my bull fell into an alder thicket that was so thick he was wedged solidly in the saplings. This was one of the heaviest elk I'd ever taken, and Murphy's Law prevailed in that the bull was lying on his belly. The alders had to be laboriously cut away, and the carcass had to be maneuvered so I could remove the entrails. This was not a happy time, and in fact, was so frustrating I can still remember the pain.

It took two full hours to position the elk, and it was long after midnight before I crawled into a sleeping bag. Two more days were needed to get the elk out of the nasty hole he fell in. On the bright side, we had horses to transport the meat. Without those

animals, a major ordeal would have been awaiting.

Sometimes Murphy stays home, and the hunting gods smile. Just recently, while hunting with Tony Knight, who invented the in-line muzzleloader, I watched Tony hit a bull in a scrub oak jungle that was so thick it defied human travel. We were standing on an old road, and when the muzzleloader belched smoke and flame I saw that it was a good hit. Instead of running deeper into the thicket, the elk ran up the slope and expired on the road we were walking on. That indeed was a stroke of very good luck. I was able to drive to the spot and we loaded the elk with no problem.

Another time I was bowhunting in Montana and hit a bull that ran 60 yards and died. He rolled down a very steep mountain for at least 400 yards and came to rest on a road. Again, I was able to drive to the bull, and smiled all the way home. But for every easy elk, I

The author carries a rack and quarter of meat in his pack for a total weight of 70 pounds.

If you have a trophy that you want mounted, you can roughly skin the cape in the field and then do the fine work when you have more time.

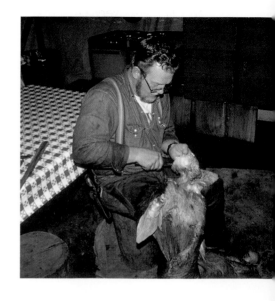

can remember a dozen that weren't.

Then there was the bull that fell six miles from my pickup. I was hunting alone, and it took me two days to pack it out. Fortunately, the weather was cool and the bears left the meat alone. I hung it in meat sacks close to where the bull fell, and packed out pieces that I could handle. As a word of advice, don't carry a load bigger than you can comfortably carry in order to cut out an extra trip. Better to walk a few more miles than hurt yourself.

If you are fortunate enough to have a horse, you can load the panniers so they're evenly balanced with meat, and proceed on a fairly easy journey out of the woods. I've had plenty of experiences with horses, some good, some not so good.

I recall a hunt with three pals where one of my friends brought two of his horses, and we rented two others. The two we rented were knot-heads in every sense of the word. I'm sure they were never in the backcountry before our hunt, and I'm also very sure that neither had ever packed elk meat. We had some very interesting little rodeos on that trip, but we were nonetheless able to make it out intact, though one of the horses was perilously close to receiving a .30/06 bullet between the eyes.

Since most hunters don't have horses, there are only a couple of other options, one of which is to carry the meat on your back. This is the worst-case scenario, and one that most of us don't look forward to. Packframes are often considered instruments of torture, especially if you're faced with a long journey out, most

I carry meat bags with me, so I can store the quarters and keep away flies.

of it uphill. I have never met a packframe that I was fond of, though some are much easier to use than others. But sooner or later, with 80 pounds or more on your back, you will develop a profound dislike for this chore and you will be able to think of nothing other than how to get rid of it.

Unfortunately, once you've reached your destination and offloaded the horrid thing on your back, you may be faced with another journey, depending on how many pals you've connived into helping you carry the meat. Sooner or later you will learn to size up your companions before planning a hunt, looking for plenty of brawn and little brains. Elk hunting with a little guy with a weak back, or even a big guy with a weak back has some serious drawbacks.

Yet another possibility is to wheel the meat out on a cart, if indeed you had the presence of mind to buy or construct a cart. When you come down to it, a wheel is one of the finest inventions mankind ever came up with. Just about everything on this earth is moved by a wheel if it moves over land. A wheeled contraption will work very nicely in the elk woods but be aware that you cannot use any wheeled devices in a wilderness area.

I carry meat bags with me, so I can store the quarters and keep away flies. If the weather is warm, flies can quickly contaminate the carcass. I'll hang the quarters in the shade, using a small portable winch to hoist them up. If you're hunting alone, you'll soon find that raising an 80- or 90-pound quarter six or seven feet off the ground is a serious task if you have no pulley system. There are of small pulleys on the market that will stow nicely in your backpack.

Another option, if you're hunting where there are plenty of roads, is to drag the elk out with a long cable attached to your vehicle. This is a slow process, but it will get your elk to a road. There is an old saying that states that the best elk is the one that falls closest to the road. Truer words have never been spoken!

PROCESSING IN THE **FIELD**

Once your elk is down you're in a battle against time. You must get it field dressed immediately, since bacteria go to work as soon as the heart stops. Every minute counts. Take pictures quickly and get to work.

Elk are gutted just like a deer, but with a lot more effort. Just the innards may weigh as much as an entire deer, and you might need to shift the elk to get at its belly. Ropes come in handy to secure it while you're working. There are several options in dealing with the carcass, depending on how far you must travel to get it out of the woods and the equipment you have, and the availability of horses. The best-case scenario is to drop the elk where you can drive to it. If you can't, then you must decide if you're going to quarter it with a saw, quarter it without a saw, or bone it.

I've boned many elk, and quartered them with a saw, but lately I've been using a different method,

called the Alaskan or Indian quartering technique. It's been around for years but is now catching on rapidly. It requires no field dressing (gutting), and no saw is required. Position the carcass on its side and skin the entire upper half, from the tail to the throat. Have someone pull on the leg so you can skin underneath it. If you have no help, use a rope by tying it to a leg, pulling it away from the body and tying the other end to a tree. Skin each leg down to the knee joint, and use the knife to sever the leg at this joint.

Sever the rear leg by cutting it from the hip all the way around. Allow the knife to follow the bone, and then pull the leg away from the carcass, which will indicate the joint. Cut through the cartilage between

These hunters are skinning a bull where it fell, cutting away the quarters and removing the rest of the meat without gutting the animal.

Put your meat in bags and hang it high to cool it in the breeze. This will also keep it out of reach of predators.

the joint and free the leg. Sever the front shoulder by making a wide cut around the shoulder bone, again pulling on the leg to help lift it off the carcass.

Cut away the backstrap, flank meat, the meat between the ribs, and the neck meat. To remove the tenderloins, which lie inside the carcass just below the spine, reach your hand in and carefully use your knife to cut the tenderloin away from the spine. This cut is accessible because the ribs end just in front of the tenderloins, allowing you to reach it. Place the chunks of meat in a game bag and put it in a shady spot.

Hang it, if possible, to allow the breeze to chill it. Make a final inspection of the carcass and be sure all the edible meat is removed. Roll the carcass over on the other side and repeat the process. When you're finished every bit of meat will be removed, and you'll leave behind only the skeleton with the innards still inside.

FREEZER TIPS

Inspect meat and trim away all fat and remove every strand of hair. Wrap each meat portion in a good quality plastic wrap. The extra cost of the wrap far outweighs the consternation of trying to work with unmanageable wrap. Be sure the wrap completely covers the meat. Place the wrapped meat in a square of quality freezer paper, and wrap securely, sealing off all air. Fasten the paper with tape. Label the meat according to the type of cut, date, and who killed the animal. Be specific. For example, don't just label backstraps as "steaks."

A big bull will weigh more than 800 pounds. If the weather is cool and you can hang it, do so, and allow it to age while you're still in the field. Remove the hide if the weather turns warm.

When initially placing meat in the freezer, don't stack it tightly, but arrange it loosely to allow the cold air to thoroughly permeate the packages.

When frozen solid, it can then be stacked tightly. Frozen meat packages are slippery and tend to slide and fall out in upright freezers. Eliminate this problem by putting the packages in a cardboard box and placing it in your freezer. Cut a U-shaped hole in the side of the box facing you so you can get your hand in and retrieve meat.

The freezer life of any meat depends on the cut, wrapping job, and length of time. I've kept elk venison in the freezer for up to three years with no obvious loss of quality, but it's best to consume the meat within a year if you can. I've found that thinner steaks tend to dry out and "burn" quicker than roasts or thicker cuts. Meat that isn't properly wrapped will "freezer burn" because air has come in contact, or it's simply been in the freezer far too long. Take good care of your meat when you process it and you'll appreciate those extra efforts at the dinner table.

INDEX